# MASTERING THE SALES RECIPE

## CREATING MEMORABLE CUSTOMER EXPERIENCES AND SALES SUCCESS

# MASTERING THE SALES RECIPE

## CREATING MEMORABLE CUSTOMER EXPERIENCES AND SALES SUCCESS

**MARK EGGERDING**

Did you enjoy the ideas, suggestions and sales success techniques in this book?

Would you like Mark Eggerding to speak to your team, company, group or organization?

Would you like additional Mastering the Sales Recipe resources to help you simplify your life and that of your customers?

Would you like additional copies of this book?

Please contact Mark at:

markeggerding.com

mark.eggerding@gmail.com

This book would never have been possible without a complement of many dear friends who encouraged me and supported me along the way. A list that includes Glen, Rae, Connor, Rabel, and the undying love of my family, Leslie, Andrew, Kyle, Adam, and Kaytlyn as well as our four wonderful grandchildren. Each of you believed in me. Thank you.

I dedicate this book completely to my best sale and love of my life, Gina.

# TABLE OF CONTENTS

**FOREWORD: CHESTER ELTON — 09**

**INTRODUCTION: A TALE OF TWO PASSIONS — 11**

**INGREDIENT 1: EMBRACE LIFE-LONG LEARNING — 17**
Learning Every Day; Back to School; What You Care About; Goal Setting; The Hardest Job in America; The Dedication Gap; Discipline; Secret Sauce

**INGREDIENT 2: COMMIT TO EXCELLENCE — 33**
Ambition; The Go-to Resource; Knowledge Is Power; Questions to Sell; Prepare and Present; Sustained Excellence; Secret Sauce

**INGREDIENT 3: UNLEASH CREATIVITY — 47**
Share a Story; Info Overload; New Customers Calls; Referrals; Rocky Times; It's About Time; Secret Sauce

**INGREDIENT 4: EXUDE FOOD-ITUDE — 63**
Warmth; Gratitude Is an Attitude; Compliments; You Need Laughter; Building on Momentum; The Inner You; Secret Sauce

**INGREDIENT 5: COMMAND CONFIDENCE — 75**
"I've Never Heard of You"; Why Buy It?; Sales and Friends; Fair-Weather Friendship; Tombstone Integrity; More Than Loyal; The Mystery of Confidence; Secret Sauce

## INGREDIENT 6: WORK SMART — 89

Catch the Confidence Bug; How to Be Interesting; Are You Happy?; Recognize Some Scary Facts; My 15 Minutes; Food Power; Fire in the Belly; Momentous Success; Your Sales Ego; Stand By; Who's the Best?; Being the Go-to; A Smile Says It All; Secret Sauce

## INGREDIENT 7: LOVE SALES — 107

Resilience; In Balance; Listen to Me; The Chain Reaction of Enthusiasm; Underground Success; Like It; The Funny; A Happy Customer Is a Satisfied Customer; A Plan of Action; Sales Smarts; Finding Attitude; Moving Onward; Secret Sauce

## MASTERING THE SALES RECIPE ACTION PLAN — 129

# FOREWORD
## CHESTER ELTON

If you sell and you want to sell more of whatever you sell in the food industry, you are going to really enjoy this book, no . . . LOVE this book. I mean it!

I have known Mark personally for several years now, and his enthusiasm for his work is contagious. Remarkably, he has been able to capture that energy in this wonderful book, *Mastering the Sales Recipe.*

When I pick up any business book to read, it has to pass three basic criteria.

1. Does the author have credibility in this space? In other words, can I trust his advice?

2. Is it readable? I have picked up books that I know have great content, but the way they are written never allows me to get past the first few chapters.

3. Does it inspire me to better performance? Will it motivate me to be better at what I do and what I love?

If it passes these three tests, I know I have a winner. A book that I will buy, read and re-read. *Mastering the Sales Recipe* is the trifecta! Mark has all the credibility in the world with his industry experience and leadership. He is one of the most trusted resources you can find.

The readability of the book is perfect. From the first section to the final paragraphs, you will find his writing style engaging, entertaining and the content practical and useful. It is real-life experience from an experienced and successful professional. It has the perfect readability for sales professionals with the short attention spans with which we are all blessed!

I love that this is not a sequenced book. As busy sales people we steal a few minutes here and there, and the way Mark makes a point in just a few pages allows you to take this book on the road and read it wherever and whenever you have a few moments and need to be inspired. It is the perfect sales companion.

If you want to be motivated to sell and build your skills, the chapters are short and to the point, the quotes are little shots of inspiration that we all need as we work the prospect and client lists. Carry it with you when you need a shot in the arm. It will be your own personal pep talk in print.

If you love selling and food, this is the book for you. So what are you waiting for? Get READING and start SELLING more and having more fun!

Turn the page already!

- Chester Elton, co-author of The New York Times Best Sellers, *The Carrot Principle* and *The Orange Revolution*.

# INTRODUCTION
## A TALE OF TWO PASSIONS

From an early age, I've loved both cooking and selling. They don't sound like they belong together, but for me these two passions have always been intertwined. My grandmother tells the story that I started my culinary career by pointing to the pots on the stove and demanding to be lifted up to see what was inside them. I was two years old at the time. When I was six, I won my first sales contest selling Christmas cards for my church. Already, I was hooked on both cooking and selling. Growing up, I alternated career paths between selling things – newspapers, light bulbs, candy bars – and cooking things.

At age 18, I started my culinary career at two restaurants in my native Cincinnati—Johnny Bench's Home Plate and Johnny Bench's Home Stretch. I began as a line cook frying fish, shrimp, and baking potatoes. What a blast and an adrenaline rush it was to be in a crowded kitchen, with orders pouring in and pressure building all around me. By 19, I was the Night Chef responsible for a crew of 40 and serving 1,000 people every night. If these customers were unhappy, my neck was on the line. I learned the importance of customer service at an early age.

I was good at what I did, but I wanted to be better. My next step was to attend the Culinary Institute of America in Hyde Park, New York to hone my culinary skills and to receive broad training in classical cuisine. Upon my return to Cincinnati, I became the Chef de Cuisine at Johnny Bench's Home Stretch. It was one of North

America's busiest and highly-rated restaurants, with the longest streak of record-breaking sales in the nation.

Of my two competing interests, I had focused on a career in cooking first, but then one day, I made a shift back to selling. I was talking to a salesperson from John Sexton & Company. Sexton had a history and reputation as impressive as Johnny Bench's. They were purveyors of fine foods, teas and coffee, beginning in 1883, and they had grown to be the leader in their field. Not long afterward, I left the kitchen to join John Sexton & Company (which later became US Foods) to pursue a career in selling the most important product in the world: food.

Immediately, I discovered that the perfectionism I learned in the kitchen was equally important in sales. As a chef, when you are in the weeds on a busy Saturday night with order dupes all over the board, you get in a mental zone and rely on your instincts and repetition of preparation to get you through it all. Every plate has to be perfect and every day needs to be better than the one before. Constant improvement has to be a chef's mantra; otherwise, he goes stale and collapses under the pressure of the kitchen. In sales, you are constantly striving to get better, too—not only to work harder every day—but to work smarter every day. A sales call or prospect meeting needs to be a mosaic of creativity, simplicity, determination, repetition, and perfection.

One of my earlier selling experiences was with Harry Panaro, a foodservice sales legend who became not only my mentor, but a trusted advisor, colleague and friend. Harry was the first sales person at John Sexton & Company to sell more than the entire sales team combined, penning more than $45 million dollars per year. He was a multiple year Presidents Cup Sales professional, held every single foodservice selling record, and was adored by his customers. He was devoted to family and country, and this was Harry's motto to live by! Harry's free spirit and creativity at an early selling age set him apart and set the stage for a life full of fun. He was a great relationship builder with a huge smile and a handshake that would warm your heart. He always enjoyed "the moment", with his customers and somehow you just felt better no matter what was happening at the time.

---

Harry taught me the power of relationship building and the value that comes from serving first, sharing what you know, and asking last.

Harry always said, "You can't take it with you, so share it with everyone." He enjoyed watching his colleagues grow in sales as well as spirit and wisdom. I was a fortunate recipient of Harry's wisdom and owe much of my career success to his early guidance and mentorship. He made me better.

I was inspired to write this book because my entire life I have been in one field or the other, cooking or selling, and I have learned that their recipes for high accomplishment are similar. Everything for both is always in motion, serving, prospecting, pitching, cooking, challenging, and creating. No matter what the product, all sales including food are always about creating memorable experiences for the customer. Food and sales are both about creating memorable experiences for the customer. Chefs and salespeople have much in common. They are both in the hospitality business. They both should be passionate, energetic, creative, competitive. To be successful, they both should love people.

Both food and selling embody my personal philosophy—"I love to serve." I am also inquisitive, which drives me to give folks a simple, fresh, different, and unique approach. I like to use experience, resources, and lessons learned from people to take old favorites and make them new, different, hip and eggcellent. (I should explain that my friends—and I hope I will be able to count you among them—call me Egg, as in short for Eggerding. Variations have evolved over the decades such as "eggcelent" and "eggstra." You may run into some of these in the coming chapters.) This is my declaration and inspiration—a rallying cry for us sales professionals and foodies at heart across the country.

The book is divided into thematic chapters. Each begins with a story from the history of food. Each includes specific tips and techniques to help you master the Seven Ingredients for Sales Success. Like a recipe, there is some overlap by design:

- Ingredient 1: Embrace Life-long Learning
- Ingredient 2: Commit to Excellence

- Ingredient 3: Unleash Creativity
- Ingredient 4: Exude Fooditude
- Ingredient 5: Command Confidence
- Ingredient 6: Work Smart
- Ingredient 7: Love Sales

Ultimately, this is more than a sales book. It is a manifesto on how the techniques of selling can be enlivened and enriched with a fresh point of view borrowed from the world of the kitchen.

These quick sales stories and lessons won't take long to read. However, it may be best to swallow the contents one ingredient at a time. In fact, I hope that you will read one per day and practice the lessons systematically and continuously. Make it a goal to perfect each one. I invite you to make a steady diet of these sales basics.

Bon appétit.

MARK EGGERDING

# INGREDIENT 1
## EMBRACE LIFE-LONG LEARNING

Revel in a sense of new-found freedom, the food will be cooked and seasoned to your own discriminating tastes. You will not only master cooking skills but go onto unexpected triumphs.

Irma Rombauer, *The Joy of Cooking*, 1936

Catherine rode in a caravan across the Italian border toward an uncertain future. She was no stranger to radical shifts of fortune. Her parents died within a few weeks of each other while she was an infant. And then she was taken in and raised by one of the wealthiest families in the history of the world—the de Medicis—the bankers of popes and kings. Now, at age fourteen, she was to be married to a man who would become the King of France. He did not love her and never would. They struggled to have children for ten years and Catherine then produced nine children, four of whom became kings and queens themselves.

Aside from the political rollercoaster that was the life of Catherine de Medici, she is regarded as one of the most important and influential figures in culinary history. How is that possible? Catherine brought with her to Paris from Florence on that nuptial journey at age fourteen a fleet of chefs and artisans who held the culinary secrets of the age. This occurred in 1533, when France was still eating heavy Medieval food; meanwhile, Italy was enjoying a burst of innovation that would change how the western world eats. These chefs brought to France new ingredients and methods of cooking them—peas, artichokes, beans, pastas, truffles, melons, veal, marmalades, ice cream, soups, pastries, custards, spices, and much more.

Catherine introduced elegance to the dinner table that included a code of manners as well as silverware, crystal, linens, and perfumes. She also introduced a newfangled tool for eating...the fork.

Think for a moment about how novel this would have been at the time. Humans had gotten along without this utensil for thousands of years. Knives descended from axes, the earliest hand tools of early man. Spoons built on whatever people could find to scoop up liquid. Humans used their hands and shells may have been an early version. Before Catherine arrived in France, many people ate with rounds of stale bread called trenchers.

Catherine never stopped learning and listening. She used public festivals and toured the country to help bridge the sectarian divisions that marked the era. Food was an integral element of these occasions when she lured members from different factions to dine together with her.

The fork, which she routinely included, was viewed suspiciously. It was considered sinister, new, and unnecessary. It was considered unmanly. And ineffective. With space between tines, what could prevent one from dropping more food that made it into one's mouth?

Catherine missed her home and family in Italy desperately. The foods and recipes from home brought her comfort and allowed the lonely, foreigner at court to become a person of influence. And she never stopped learning and applying her knowledge. Among other things, she wielded equal power over fashion, dance, and decoration. She modernized eating and entertaining, and she made French food international. She was a turning point for gastronomy, and—through the eventual acceptance of the fork—she used a passion for learning about food and people and changed the way millions of people have eaten ever since, including you.

When people ask me what it takes to be successful in the world of sales, I think of the knowledge that Catherine de Medici brought to France. I am inspired by her embracing change and envisioning opportunities no one had seen before. There are lessons to be learned from her experience and influence. Even though the future queen had money and power, she reached inside to leverage a drive to never stop learning and achieve something lasting.

Among other qualities, Catherine made a commitment to discovering new things constantly. She embraced the new. Instead of isolating herself in a new land and a new position, she demonstrated pride in her heritage and was eager to share it with others, however hostile they might have been initially. She showed a dedication to the ideas about which she was passionate. As we mentioned, the French derided the fork when Catherine introduced it at court. They thought it was stupid and the men considered it effeminate. This attitude lasted a generation after Catherine, until Louis XIV. As queen, she remained a student of those who could provide valuable expertise. And finally, she showed great discipline in the face of adversity. This was not a woman who allowed others to limit what she was capable of achieving.

You are not setting goals to be the kings and queens of France, but this chapter does point to ways that you can be ruler over your own destiny in the profession of sales by embracing life-long learning as a core ingredient to your success.

# LEARNING EVERY DAY

The salesperson has a crazy job description. In short it is this: be able to walk up to anybody, anywhere, and start a conversation that engages him or her on the things they care most about. If everyone had the same ten interests, it would be easy. Instead, we meet people from a multitude of cultures who have varied passions and skills. Some respond to humor, others dislike it; some are all business; others want to be friends first. Even regarding products that we are selling, some people already know a lot about them and others are novices. Personalities, background, education, interests: whoever the person, there is a key that unlocks the door to a potential connection between them and us.

The salesperson's job is so challenging because, realistically, there is no way one person can know everything necessary to engage everyone in the world. And yet, that is the potential of our job. The only solution is that a sales profession must commit to continuous learning. Every day presents a new opportunity to gather information that we can stash away for a future need. We must always be open to a creative way to apply that learning in new situations to engage prospects and customers.

Surprisingly, many salespeople are like gliders that get up to speed and then coast along peacefully. Sales isn't about coasting. We need propulsion to succeed, and I've found that information equals momentum.

In addition to the obvious advice—learn people's names, know your product, understand every facet of your business—learning also extends to sports, pop culture, local, national and international issues, the arts, jokes, weather, and on and on. Anything that an existing or potential customer might find interesting—that's your target of learning. I read a daily paper. I listen to the radio and podcasts. I follow blogs and social media. I talk to people about what is going on around them. I try to pick up phrases in foreign languages. I don't love talking about politics, religion, and other issues that are polarizing, but I keep abreast of those topics because people expect it from someone who is well-informed. Even though I don't follow every sporting event, I have areas of expertise and a passing knowledge of who is playing whom. I do the same with food and food trends, movies, books, television, music, performing arts, science, and technology.

It's easy to be knowledgeable about things you already know (that sounds redundant, but you know what I mean). The trick is to broaden your base of expertise. Such a goal can only be reached if you commit to learning every day.

# BACK TO SCHOOL

I clearly remember my first day back at school each year. Don't you? As soon as I stepped into the classroom each autumn, it all felt both new and familiar. There were new faces and old friends, former teachers and future teachers, skills I had mastered and ideas yet to discover.

There's a distinct energy in the air on the first day of school. Some of it is fear, I suppose. Potential humiliations, failures, and tensions lurk around the corner, but more importantly, students sense that something new and maybe even great is about to happen.

Whether you are the kind of person who likes to look back or is more focused on the future, there are moments when it is great to reassess where you are and focus on what you want. It's a back-to-school moment. Some people reassess where they are on the first day of the new year, others on their birthday. I know people who look at Monday mornings as a mini-assessment time. Whatever time you choose to reevaluate, take a moment and renew your commitment to your goals. Look at where you are, what you know, and what you care most about. Let each of those reflections drive what you do next.

Where You Are. When students come back to school, teachers give them exams to reassess their understanding (and to see how much they've forgotten over the summer). Regarding your goals, ask yourself where you stand in the process of achievement. What have you done so far? Are you on track? What processes need realignment?

What You Know. After you recognize what it is you have learned, it will be clearer that there is much you have yet to learn. I think that there is a big connection between learning and change. When something new comes my way—whether that's a new fact, a new face, or a new experience—I am forced to adapt. Without change, we don't learn. As you consider your goals, try to pinpoint the gaps. What more can you discover?

# WHAT YOU CARE ABOUT

In school, I always did best in subjects that I liked the best, not the other way around. Being a master of a subject is empowering and energizing. In the old days, masters took apprentices under their wing to learn a trade. After years of watching, learning, and trying, the apprentices attempted to show that they were ready to go it alone. They created a masterpiece, something like a master's thesis project. This masterpiece was intended to say to the world, "I am ready." How do you know if you have mastered your skill? Knowledge, competence, success, and passion are all ingredients of mastery. The dirty little secret of mastery is this: there's no such thing; you're never done learning.

A day does come, however, when you feel confident to share what you know with others. Just like the teacher in front of the classroom who is still learning herself, you owe it to others to pass on what you know. Find someone to mentor, engage with your peers, write, present, and spread the word.

Today is a back-to-school day. Right now, where are you, what do you know, what have you still to learn, and how can you pass it on?

# GOAL SETTING

Salespeople are goal people. We thrive on benchmarks, measureable progress, comparisons, challenges, and motivation. While other people scribble down a few New Year's resolutions and then promptly fall off the wagon, sales folks think strategically about goals. For us, goals are serious business.

I think one of the reasons why people in the sales profession respond so strongly to the idea of goal setting is the simple fact that our job is tough. There are a million reasons not to try. As I like to say, the hardest door to open is your own car door; it takes courage to leave a safe space and to put yourself out in front of the public. We get pushed back, knocked down, rejected. All of that negativity would be overwhelming if it weren't for the bigger picture and the realization that every day has the potential of bringing us a bit closer to our main purpose.

It is a mistake to think of goal setting as a once-a-year activity. Milestone dates are logical moments to stop and reflect, but any time is the right time to articulate your ambitions and make a plan to reach them. If you think about it, goal setting is breakthrough thinking. You need to give yourself some contemplative time to collect your thoughts. Here are a few techniques that I've used.

- Take an hour to jot down thoughts about what you want to accomplish
- Focus on them, even if it takes a few days to do it
- As you review, develop a few points of action, at least one for each goal
- Pick an action, including the techniques that will make it work
- Implement it
- Note how the new behavior improves your performance
- Tinker with the recipes, so to speak, to hone in on exact actions to ideally reach your aspirations.

Your goals are likely focused on yourself, your success, your rewards, your progress. But what about your customers? Imagine going to them, and sitting down to discuss with them their goals. Do that. Make an appointment and review with customers what they want to accomplish. Then, ask them how you can help. This is a simple exercise, but few people do it.

What's important to remember about goals is that they are rarely mutually exclusive between parties. It isn't about a winner and a loser. When you express a willingness to help the customer reach a goal, a bond is formed. That trust will translate to future success for you both.

Finally, use your time to set goals for yourself as a brainstorming exercise for your customer. Write down ideas that will give new options for your customer, provide renewed focus for them, and recharge their drive to excel. This will offer you clues on how to proceed. They will respond with loyalty, and they will be willing to take a chance on future ideas that you present. You are sowing the seeds of future success. That's your goal.

# THE HARDEST JOB IN AMERICA

Each year, Manpower, Inc., a global leader in Human Resources lists the "hardest jobs to fill in America." Consistently, Sales Reps have ranked in the top five. A couple of years, we were No. 1. Salespeople are hard to find. Great sales people are the rarest of the rare.

I sometimes wonder why it is that sales is so tough. Ultimately, it comes down to the skill set needed to excel. It requires extraordinary resilience, a broad range of knowledge, superior communication talents, a high degree of self-motivation, and an uncanny balance—something like a sixth sense—of unwritten codes.

I can think of seven traits off the top of my head that are prerequisites to being a sales superstar. Maybe someone possessing these qualities would succeed at anything they tried, but it seems to me that the sum total of them is a checklist for the hardest job in America.

- Salespeople are self-aware. They have a solid identity of who they are, in terms of both as strengths and weaknesses; they may be ambitious, but they are also reasonable about what they can achieve and why they want to achieve it.
- Salespeople are patient, in a persistent sort of way. It is a question of understanding a client; they can tune in to what the customer is thinking and they can lay the groundwork for eventual success even if it does not look initially promising.
- Salespeople are smart, but they make it look easy. I think of it as a high level of being comfortable and confident; they know everything there is to know about their product, but when they talk about it, the discussion never feels rote or canned. They thrive on staying ahead of the curve.
- Salespeople are people-persons. More than any industry I can think of, sales personnel genuinely like to be around other people; they see them as peers, and as a result, they can get to the emotional aspect of connecting with others through their empathy for them.
- Salespeople are problem-solvers. It's almost a game for salespeople, they love a challenge, they are able to anticipate roadblocks, and they look forward to finding answers for others.
- Salespeople know how to be persuasive without being pushy. Sales people intuitively know how to find common ground with customers. Rather than assigning judgment when there is disagreement, sales people naturally want to see all points of view. They can clearly espouse their own ideas without belittling other viewpoints.
- Salespeople are future-focused. Partly as a competitive strategy but also a personality trait, sales attracts professionals who are optimistic, who plan ahead, and who can

forecast where they need to be next in order to be in the middle of the action.

Sales is a noble profession. It's hard. And there are many people who simply can't do it. That's why it's so tough to find sales people. Those who wish to tackle the challenges set themselves apart from the rest. That's something to be proud of.

# THE DEDICATION GAP

Working for peanuts!
In searching for a replacement crop for cotton to help farmers who had lost everything due to boll weevil infestations, George Washington Carver discovered the power of the peanut. He became an advocate of peanut cultivation and consumption, publishing 105 ways for using the peanut in 1916. But he didn't stop there; by the end of his career he had developed more than 300 peanut products well beyond the edible, including wallboard, paints, soaps and dyes.

It always surprises me, as I talk to some people, to hear how they expect everything to be handed to them merely because they say they want it. All of us have heard the "follow your dream" sermon so often that we can be forgiven for imagining that any desire can be easily attained by wishing for it. We watch overnight sensations on television and come to expect that we deserve instant success too.

The profession of sales is equally full of people who have unrealistic expectations. They want it so badly. They want it. They must have it! What is "it", exactly? I assume that they are referring to all of the rewards of success. It's funny though because I don't see it that way at all.

Sometimes I imagine these people walking up to a rock star after a concert and saying, "Hey, you're great. I want what you have." The star-struck fan would probably be horrified to hear about all the music lessons, the hours of practice, the attempts to be heard, the rejections, the performances at lousy venues, the loneliness of travel, and so on. The "it" is pretty great for a rock star, but you don't get it in a day.

I've been fortunate in sales and have earned "it." But just like the concert musician, I've paid my dues and learned my lessons. If someone were to walk up to me and say, "Hey, you're great. I want what you have", I'd make a list of things that they have to do to earn it.

First of all, success is a byproduct of skill. Wanting is not a skill, it's a motivation. The acquisition of skill is paramount to sales success. There are specific tools, methods, approaches, and techniques in the sales profession. When I was just starting out, I had a powerful mentor who explained these things—and better yet, showed me these things. The lessons didn't sink in immediately. It took time and practice, failure and disappointment, but ultimately, I learned how to sell.

Another word for it is dedication. It is the determined manifestation of desire. The way I see it, there is a dedication gap today. It is as if we are increasingly impatient and want a shortcut for everything worthwhile in our lives. People want success and instinctively they know they're not fully prepared, but they assume that a strong desire and aggressive self-confidence will compensate for it. And you know what, sometimes it does work out that way. We call that luck. But for anyone who wants great achievement, dedication becomes the foundation for its longevity.

Want it, yes, but make a plan, learn the skills, follow a role model. And don't stop.

# DISCIPLINE

Talented people make it all look so easy. A jazz pianist improvising in a nightclub, a public speaker standing in front of a crowd without prepared notes, an actor ad-libbing to cover for the flubbed line of a colleague, a basketball star who sinks a last-second shot from half court, a police detective who finds evidence everyone else missed, a surgeon who mends the heart of an infant in utero: all make superhuman feats look like child's play.

Such achievement is more than mere repetition and practice. Many kids play little league baseball, after all, who never get drafted into the major leagues. What is it then that transforms interest and desire into something higher?

I thought of this recently after reading of the extraordinary accomplishment of Geoffry Mutai, the Kenyan runner who completed the Boston Marathon with the fastest time of any runner in history. He ran the 2011 race in 2 hours, 3 minutes, and 2 seconds. Do the math. That's an average of under 4.7 minutes per mile for 26.2 miles. In the last Olympics, the gold medalist crossed the finish line in 2:06:32. How is it possible that humans can do that?

To my mind, the key is discipline. Cynical people might counter that genetics play a larger role. There's an old joke: If you want to win a gold medal at the Olympics, choose your parents wisely; I disagree. People who excel at something become great because they take whatever natural gifts they possess and amplify them with strategic effort.

If someone desires to be a world-class salesperson, he or she might think that they can simply turn on the charm and use whatever innate gifts they have to win people over. In the short-term, such an approach might pan out okay. But when tough competition shows up and when dozens of unfamiliar scenarios appear, winging it won't work. Instead, the salesperson who aspires to be best-in-class needs to train for it.

Think of the skill you worked on the hardest growing up (getting good grades, being good at sports, music, etc.,) and approach sales just as systematically. Learn everything about sales. Read the best books, talk to experts, watch and learn. Discover as much as you can about the product you want to sell. Know its history, how it works, and why people respond to it. Be aware of the emotional connections between people and the thing you wish to sell. Figure out exactly how to tell its story, that is, how to explain to people why your product matters. All of these things (and countless other points of expertise) require sustained, focused effort. Be disciplined about the acquisition of that knowledge. Make a list of things you need to learn, make a plan regarding your education of it, and doggedly train for success. Don't let anything distract you. Think of your goal as your mission and dedicate yourself to it. That's how people succeed.

# SECRET SAUCE

Let's review the main points of this chapter:

Sales is about propulsion, not gliding. The fuel is continuous learning.

By assessing where you are and what you know, you can plan what's next.

You will like best that which you know best.

Goals are achieved by those who consciously make them.

Sales is one of the hardest jobs in America, but it is a noble profession.

The gap between where you are and where you want to be is bridged by discipline.

The U.S. Bureau of Labor Statistics lists over 14 millions salespeople in the United States. That number is skewed large because it includes anyone working behind a cash register, but still, sales as a profession is massive. Furthermore, few people are academically trained for their jobs the way they might be if they labored in advertising, plumbing, acting, or journalism. There is a gap, then, of information and expertise for the contemporary sales professional. Perhaps this is one reason why so many of us in sales are constantly striving to learn new techniques, approaches, and strategies for getting better at what we do.

Over time, this habit of learning becomes ingrained behavior. Maybe it starts with a feeling of inadequacy, but for us, learning grows to be a life-long adventure. I am referring to something larger than sales technique here. Learning for its own sake comes to be fun and as vital in our jobs as breathing. Why? Sales professionals cannot hide in an office or do the same job over and over. We are out in the field, talking, shaking hands, making contacts, introducing ourselves, attempting to stand out in a crowded field of competitors. Every piece of information or trivia or experience we gather can be used to break the ice, establish camaraderie, and build trust.

Learning, then, becomes our currency. When we invest in ourselves by learning new things, we can be sure it will pay dividends professionally.

Another reason to be a life-long learner: in an industry changing as rapidly as ours, each of us simply must be dedicated to staying abreast of new things. Innovations in the ways we communicate, for example, has transformed every aspect of our lives. Certainly it has affected our sales lives radically. Can you imagine a sales person today who decided, on New Year's Day that he would no longer learn anything new? Would that person be able to compete right now? I don't think so.

I'm reminded of the oft-quoted remark by Albert Einstein, "Wisdom is not a product of schooling but the life-long attempt to acquire it."

# INGREDIENT 2
## COMMIT TO EXCELLENCE

Good food is the foundation of genuine happiness.
Auguste Escoffier

As a young boy, he showed promise as an artist, and his family assumed he would be a painter or sculptor. But when he was thirteen, Auguste Escoffier went to work as an apprentice in his uncle's restaurant in Nice, France, and that started the remarkable career of the "king of chefs and chef of kings." For us today, the accomplishments of Escoffier that set him apart as more than a historical footnote are the groundbreaking ways he altered what we eat and how it is prepared and served. No chef in history has had more influence in the restaurant kitchen. He was a one-man food revolution.

Throughout his life, every work experience translated into a dramatic rethinking of food. His commitment to excellence and transformation is astounding. He was relentlessly innovative, both in the food he cooked and in the business of cooking. As a soldier in the Franco-Prussian War, for example, he was assigned to prepare meals for soldiers. This led Escoffier to a study of putting food in tins and jars, the first chef to seriously study canning.

Upon his return from the war, he worked in a series of restaurant kitchens. The conditions were terrible. To be a chef was not a respected career at the beginning of the twentieth century. Chefs slaved in horrible, violent, chaotic, and unsanitary conditions. The style of French food at the time relied upon the fussy, haute cuisine of chef Marie-Antoine Carême, and although the elaborate dishes were amazing to behold, they were torturous to prepare.

Escoffier, as he rose to positions of influence, changed all of that. He modernized the menu by streamlining it and by clearing away ostentation. He used seasonal foods and sauces that were lighter and healthier. He preserved the nutritional value of foods. He created the a la carte menu. He wrote books on food that are still in use today, principally, the masterful *Le Guide Culinaire* (1903). He organized the kitchen by tasks to be performed, perhaps his most revolutionary contribution to restaurant life. The brigade system reorganized the kitchen from a single unit of overlapping labor to a compartmentalized factory where each cook worked at a specific post: fish here, meat there, dessert over there, and so forth—each supervised by an autonomous *chef de partie* or station chef.

He became famous, rich (as he joined Cesar Ritz, the founder of the Ritz Hotel chain), and highly decorated. He received the cross of the Legion d'Honneur—the highest decoration in France—in 1919, the first chef to receive such recognition. His commitment to excellence never waned, and as his reputation grew, he used his influence to develop food-related charities for the hungry and philanthropies for aging chefs.

I am in the food business, and I admire Escoffier greatly as a chef and as a human being. And I am in the sales business, and I am astounded by Escoffier's ability to react to his environment, to see what his customers needed, and to revolutionize the methods to deliver excellence. In this chapter, you'll find articles about ambition, excellence, being the go-to resource, expertise, and other topics that explore how anyone in sales can develop the traits necessary to take their work to the next level of greatness through the essential ingredient of a commitment to excellence.

# AMBITION

In the days of Colonial America, a young Benjamin Franklin lived in Philadelphia where he struggled to make a living. Long before his days as a politician and elder statesman, Franklin ran a small printshop in the same space where he also ate and slept. He confronted a long list of economic challenges, but despite them his friends knew he was destined for success. Even more than success, they predicted greatness for him. They made such a bold call in part because of Franklin's extraordinary work ethic. He was endlessly curious, tirelessly innovative, and boundlessly ambitious.

Every project Franklin undertook in his shop was begun with a singular commitment to success. His abilities as a printer shone. His product was superior to his competitors' because he was determined to make it superior. He was shrewd in his business practices as well. It became clear to everyone around him that Franklin would not settle for average, for mere survival. He seemed on a clear trajectory to run his own printing company one day, which eventually, he did. Of course, history knows that he went much further still. He famously said, "All mankind is divided into three classes: those that are immovable, those that are movable, and those that move." Franklin was a mover.

Of the many lessons to be learned from Benjamin Franklin, sales professionals would be wise to hone in on the power of ambition and how it relates to skill. In my opinion, there is such a thing as empty ambition. I define it as people who sit in a chair and want something badly, but not so much that they get out of the chair (and years later, the energy that might have been deployed to be successful is spent in soothing acts of self-justification). I can't imagine Franklin ever met a challenge that way, and neither should you. Instead, use your ambition to propel yourself to action, specifically to acquire the skills necessary to be better than your competitors in sales.

Use your ambition to:

- Bring something unique to the marketplace,
- Convey something that will make people remember who you are, and
- Elevate you above your competitors.

# THE GO-TO RESOURCE

Trust is earned. Here are two quick stories to illustrate the point.

Potatoes, formerly distrusted, became popular in the late 16th century among Spanish villagers when it helped them survive major military campaigns. Potatoes, growing beneath the ground, escaped soldiers' pillaging. It took the Seven Years War (1756-1763) to get real believers into the potato camp, however, when potatoes, planted at Frederick the Great's (King of Prussia's) urging in the 1740's, sustained the peasant farmers and ensured the survival of the Prussian state.

Furthering the cause was Antoine-Augustin Parmentier, a French scientist captured by the Prussians, who spent three years as a POW eating nothing but potatoes. He convinced the scientific community of its nutritional benefits, but people were still skeptical. His publicity stunts in 1785 worked brilliantly. First, he served potatoes to Louis XVI and Marie Antoinette and obtained their royal endorsement. Then he posted armed guards around fields just outside of Paris where potatoes were being grown, making the locals curious. When the crop was ready, he withdrew the armed guards and locals rushed in to steal the potatoes, considering them valuable enough to need guarding—once used, they were convinced by the tubers' versatility and taste.

In the rest of Europe, opposition melted away by the 1790's after bad wheat harvests forced farmers to consider alternative crops.

Today, the nutritional value of the potato is sustaining populations in developing countries in South Asia and Africa. And, of course, potatoes in a variety of forms, are a favorite in America and other countries. As M. F. K. Fisher wrote in *How to Cook a Wolf*, "Potatoes are one of the last things to disappear, in times of war, which is probably why they should not be forgotten in times of peace."

Henry John Heinz built his company on transparency and trust. His first product was horseradish in a clear glass bottle, issued in 1869. Competitors extended their horseradish with fillers, concealed from view in green glass jars, Heinz took his stand on quality and proudly displayed his product in transparent bottles...no leaves, wood fiber or turnip filler. The food processing industry was young at this time, and commercial preservation in cans and bottles had yet to earn the public trust.

When I hear people talking about sales, I notice that they emphasize the motivation of our personnel. They speak as though all it takes to be successful is to have unending reservoirs of drive. Obviously, being internally motivated is one of the powerful traits of anyone in sales. It isn't enough.

Sometimes we talk about the profession of sales as if success is a water well that the motivated person can reach if they dig deeply enough, and then continue to tap at will. Personally, I would like to hear more about what someone in sales can do for a customer. That is the real world proposition because when it comes down to it, a customer has more than one option. A sales professional can push and push, be charming, act like your best friend, and so on, but ultimately the customer's decision to buy from you or someone else will be based on the value that you provide.

When I think of being a go-to resource, I recall the people in my life whom I trusted most—people who always watched out for me, who had the answers, and who would go beyond expectations to help me. Those are qualities that inspire. If salespeople truly want to be great, they will be indispensable. They will be the first person whom customers think of when they are in need.

In your marketplace, whatever that is, you can build your brand as a go-to resource. First, construct a reputation as a salesperson who is passionate, not about making a sale, but about the product and service. Next, control the message and monetize it. Years ago, there were fewer sources of information, but access to technology gives any customer a broad base of alternatives, now. You can distinguish yourself as a filter of information overload if you know everything there is to know about your product, but more importantly, everything that the customer needs to know to profit from your product.

Thirdly, you must be memorable. In order to be the go-to person, the customer has to know who you are, and the association with your name must be positive. Think of it as a story you are telling about yourself. Every interaction you have with a customer is a chapter in that story. You control it. Yes, mistakes happen and bad times cycle in and out; you can't foresee everything, but you can control the way you react and serve the customer. Sometimes, a bad day handled expertly is the best story of all.

Lastly, a go-to resource is always ready. There is no downtime. A customer expects to pick up the phone and have you on the other end. If not, the customer can go to the next name on the list. More than phone access, this concept of being ready pervades everything we do. It isn't a burden of time management or work/life balance, it is an opportunity to be of value and to prove our worth to others.

# KNOWLEDGE IS POWER

Imagine that you are listening to two salespeople giving a pitch. One talks on and on about himself, and the other talks about you. Which is more appealing?

500 years ago, a British philosopher said, "Knowledge is power."

That phrase should be a mantra for every salesperson. It can refer to knowledge about the product—that is something I emphasize often—but knowledge about the customer is equally powerful. Here are three tools to attain and use information to your advantage about the people whom you serve.

Search. Obviously, you are going to Google or otherwise research prospects and customers. The information you discover will help you see, in broad strokes, how to calibrate your message. But don't stop there. A cursory search will only give you surface information. In addition to the person's name and business, add keywords that could give a hint to other useful data, such as "awards" or even "lawsuits." Seek out information from business journals and local records. These will usually lead to additional sources of background.

You're not a stalker, you're discovering these facts so you can engage the person as fully as you can. If you have insight into his or her passions and activities, that knowledge is useful. You will discover things you have in common, people you both know, interests you share. Don't assume that once you've gathered data, you're done. There is no such thing as being always up-to-date.

Networking. Every industry is like a little community. People know each other, have histories together, and share common goals. Use these overlapping networks to bring yourself up to speed on your prospects and customers. Association meetings, networking events, professional organization functions, even sponsored charities and sporting events provide opportunities to gather intelligence and to make connections.

When you do bump into the people you want to meet, don't do the majority of the talking. Pull back and listen. After a conversation ends, take notes, if necessary, on items that you want to follow up on. Be an active participant in discussions, but keep an ear open for new knowledge.

I should add a word about gossip. You will encounter, as you seek knowledge, unsavory facts about people. Bad news is easier to find than good. Be careful. Don't dismiss negative stories;

rather, investigate them enough to discover whether they are wrong. But true or false, it is wrong of you to gossip about it. It is also professional suicide. You have nothing to gain as a salesperson by having such a reputation. Salespeople are natural talkers; stop talking about gossip. To commandeer the WWII spy warning, "Loose lips lose (sales) slips."

Speak their lingo. After you have a foundation of knowledge, either about a person or a common interest, reflect your understanding by speaking as an insider. That is, talk like they talk. Use their technical terms, acronyms, and buzzwords. Refer to the players and their milestones with ease and assurance. These verbal touches send a message: "I'm one of you. You can trust me." When prospects or customers believe that you understand them, then they will be more open to your message.

Sales professionals sometimes will resist all of the above. They will say they don't have the time necessary to research. I understand their concern, but knowledge truly is power, and research is a crop that yields great harvests.

# QUESTIONS TO SELL

Repeatedly, as I work with customers, I've discovered that asking questions is the gateway to everything that is to follow. If knowledge empowers, then the logical first step is to ask questions that will give you knowledge. I know that sounds very elementary, but I am continually surprised how rarely salespeople ask questions that effectively convert to closing a deal. More specifically, I hear a lot of questions that are wasteful and even lazy. They show a lack of preparation and an almost prodigal squandering of opportunity. More than merely asking questions, asking the right question shows in an instant that you are worthy of the customer's attention. This one skill will distinguish you from the pack.

I am reminded of the old movie, *The Pink Panther Returns*. One of my favorite exchanges is the following:

Clouseau: Does your dog bite?

Hotel clerk: No.

Clouseau: Nice doggie. (Bowing down to pet the dog. Dog barks and bites Clouseau in the hand.) I thought you said your dog did not bite!

Hotel clerk: That is not my dog.

Almost as inept, if less comical, are the conversations I overhear between mediocre salespeople and their customers. As they try to engage customers, the salesperson says, "Tell me about your business" or worse, "Let me tell you about myself." Imagine instead what kind of response you would get if you asked a potential customer this question, "Who's been your favorite customer so far today?" It is a stark difference, isn't it? Questions like these indicate that you really care, that you speak the same language, that you want to experience things from the customer's viewpoint, and that you are willing to be creative and potentially come up with solutions to problems in new ways.

Before you ask even one more pointless question, do these three things:

- Create a list of about a dozen great, open-ended questions that are tailored to reveal a customer's needs.
- Learn to watch and listen in order to pick up verbal and non-verbal cues on how to proceed with the next question.
- Keep an eye on your tone and your body language. Intuitively, the customer can tell how sincere you are, and the best question in the world can't work if you ask it without genuine curiosity.

# PREPARE AND PRESENT

I look at every customer as an ongoing opportunity rather than a one-time sale. I think of sales as a continuous activity. Each sales call gives me the chance to renew relationships and deepen them, to provide solutions, answer questions, and to inspire and educate. With so much riding on a sales call, I can't leave it to chance. Walking into such a meeting unprepared is like a basketball player who refuses to learn the team plays; he relies on innate talent and hopes that he can wing it.

Here's a better way. Think of your regularly scheduled sales meeting as an eight-step process from preparation to presentation. Take care to fully develop each step to maximize its effectiveness.

- Before you sit down for a meeting with a customer, review your notes of the last call. This will give you a roadmap.
- Chart out a positive vision for the meeting. Even the most perfunctory sales call can blow up in your face if you don't have a plan.
- Once you're there, quickly recap your common goals. These should be both short-term and long-term objectives.
- In the marketplace, since your last meeting, there will have been changes, challenges, and new products. Review them together and determine whether a new product could add value for your customer.
- At the end of the last meeting, you will have left an idea for something you thought would be profitable for the customer. Discuss the customer's thoughts since you last met regarding your idea.
- Present ideas to the customer and focus on the person's physical involvement such as giving them a sample to open, handing them a point of sale, etc. Your goal is to replace passive listening with mutual engagement.
- Based on the research you've done in advance, inspire the

customer by sharing ideas that are topical and customer-specific. If you can consistently bring new and exciting ideas to the table when you have a sales call with the customer, he or she will look forward to seeing you.
- After the meeting, keep a record of the discussion including points to follow-up and research. This will give you an advantage when you circle back for your next sales call.

# SUSTAINED EXCELLENCE

In the business world, a commitment to excellence is something that is discussed more frequently in manufacturing than in sales. It's unfortunate. Generally speaking, excellence translates into longevity. When something is accomplished that is excellent, the thing—the object, the idea, the relationship—endures better than something that is seen as useful but disposable.

I want to be successful and I want you to be successful, not as a one-time event, but for the long haul. This kind of sustainability can only happen when you commit to excellence. While there are certainly examples of business plans built upon obsolescence (there is a reason that coffee is not sold in fine china mugs, let's say), at the heart of business is the prerequisite notion that everything you do has to be designed to fit the challenge at hand as perfectly as possible.

In sales, that means that losing a client is an imperfect act. Squandering leads and showing up to meetings unprepared are small but notable failures. Lazy questions and haphazard record-keeping are likewise indicators that you're not committed to being the best. This is not excellence.

All of these examples are tools. I think that one of the reasons why being in sales is so difficult is that the profession is under-trained. People want to be successful and they bring to sales great enthusiasm, but systemically, we have lost sight of the tools of the trade. Years ago, new salespeople followed a mentor around. We watched what worked and didn't work. We learned how to be excellent by patterning behavior of those who had already accomplished excellence. The realities of the marketplace today are frequently different from that idea. It isn't uncommon to hear about a new salesperson who arrives on the job, is given an area to work, a stack of things to sell, and is sent out to sink or swim alone. We shouldn't be surprised at the high burnout rate in our profession.

I am advocating something quite different. If organizations have fewer means to train a salesforce, then the sales professionals themselves have to compensate. This puts the burden on the individual, true, but it also provides unique competitive advantages if the individual is willing to get really good at the art of the sale.

There is a moment when everyone new to sales decides whether they will limp along or go for it all. For someone who aspires to excellence, which pays dividends longer and more forcefully than simply being good enough, it all begins with a declaration that you will be better informed, more knowledgeable, better prepared, more solidly devoted, more curious, better able to serve and inspire than anyone else. That is excellence, and that is what will reward you longer than anything else.

# SECRET SAUCE

Let's review the main points of this chapter:

Ambition can fuel innovation and propel you to new achievements.
For superior sales results, become the go-to resource for your customers.
In your toolbox, nothing is more powerful than knowledge.
A great question posed to a customer transforms the relationship.
Prepare for your sales calls; never wing it.

---

Excellence is entirely up to you.

Every non-fiction, self-help book in the world follows the same format: identify the problem, then find the solution. It's a simple thing. I am not the first author to tell a reader that they have the power to be better than they are, to know more than they currently know.

If this concept is already out there in the world, why do you need someone else to remind you of its worth? Because excellence is hard work. It requires commitment. And there's no single best way to achieve it. You try one approach. You squeeze all you can from it, and then you try another, and another. You may be motivated to progress today, but after a setback, resolve weakens. And then you find another motivator, and you begin again.

Likewise, strategies and techniques necessarily evolve and change as the landscape shifts under your feet, but the underlying motivation is more constant: to be excellent in your life.

Henry David Thoreau, the philosopher/day-camper at Walden Pond, once said, "Rather than love, than money, than fame, give me truth." Ummm, ok, but I wouldn't mind a little love, a little money, and a little fame. The truth is that all of us have ambitions and only some of us pursue them with dogged determination. I would take it further. I believe that anyone who has truly become excellent at something has had to approach the seemingly impossible job one step at a time. Excellence is not handed to you. It isn't achieved by dreaming about it either. There's no recipe for excellence that doesn't require work.

# INGREDIENT 3
## UNLEASH CREATIVITY

> To entertain successfully one must create with the imagination of a playwright, plan with the skill of a director, and perform with the instincts of an actor.
> James Beard, American cook, author, TV personality

In the years leading up to 1900, if patrons of fine food wanted a luxurious meal, they found it . . . near a train. Few people today realize that the history of upscale dining in America owes much to the entrepreneurs George Pullman, Fred Harvey, and others who introduced passengers to pampered eating as they traveled great distances on the rails.

Pullman, an engineer, introduced the "hotel car" in 1867 which would become known as the Pullman sleeping car. It was a converted sleeper that featured a limited range of dining. The following year, he launched a dining car, the Delmonico, named after the most famous restaurant of its time, located in Manhattan. Pullman laid the groundwork for a rapid expansion of possibilities of railroad restaurant dining. Fred Harvey followed suit, and in 1892, his railroad depot restaurants included the Santa Fe, and the trains The California Limited, and The Super Chief. Soon, every rail line was trying to best the competition with elevated service, and that meant great food.

Imagine the planning required to serve a fine meal to elite customers aboard a train. Fresh fish lay in refrigerators in ice chips, local ingredients were purchased along the route, bins were filled with drinks, humidors held cigarettes and fine cigars. Trains had the equivalent of root cellars to preserve vegetables. Meats were cut, inspected and wrapped in advance. And prep kitchens were organized to use every possible inch of available space.

This was more than just serving food. These trains aspired to serving great food. They offered delicacies such as oysters and salmon, fine cuts of beef, lamb and veal. Fruits and vegetables were locally sourced and picked fresh. Food was served on fine linen, with heavy silver, beautiful stemware, and silver-plated china. Diners were exposed to new ingredients from the regions that the trains serviced. Some signature dishes were found only aboard trains, including Shoo-Fly Pie (Pennsylvania Railroad), Georgia Peaches (Southern Railway), and Golden Dollar French Toast (Missouri Pacific).

Chefs for dining cars were lured away from leading hotels. They became the chef-stars of their day, used in promotional materials and advertising. The kitchens themselves became factories of innovation. With their limited space, they were early adopters of electricity and technologies that were developed for submarines. Scheduling was complex as well. As the train traveled, dining cars were decoupled and serviced, restocked, and then sent en route in different directions to care for other guests. This revolution in fine dining was only possible because of detailed planning, rigorous learning, and innovative thinking. There were simply too many logistical variables otherwise.

Like the tastemakers of the day, every Sales professional who desires true innovation and breakthrough success must be equally focused on planning and doing their homework. This chapter includes a menu of ideas that can help you navigate your way to success through unleashing creativity.

# SHARE A STORY

One of the most extraordinary characteristics of Americans is our ability to think inventively. We are creative and ambitious. If we have enough drive, Americans are free to learn and grow and innovate their way to success. Our nation's history is replete with famous inventors. Think of the objects you use in a single day and trace back their histories. Many of these things—cars, electricity, telecommunications, medicines, technology, and so much more— were born in the U.S.A.

If we represent the land of free choice and the home base for invention, we are equally good at storytelling. This is true in a literal way, with Hollywood and the publishing and the music industries leading the way in global entertainment production, but it is also true of individuals and organizations. We know how to tell our own stories. We have always been adept at keeping our own history and turning that into a media message.

Those two characteristics, invention and storytelling, are related in business and particularly in sales. The notion of pairing a sales-person and a story might strike you as suspect. I'm not suggesting that we make up stories, or fabricate untruths as part of our busi-ness.

This kind of storytelling is completely different. Each of us is in charge of our own branding. We present a message to the world of ourselves. That story can be elaborate or simple, but it tells peo-ple a great deal about us.

As we sell, we are telling a story. It is the story of a product, what it does, where it came from, and what it can do for a customer. Un-like a list of factoids and statistics, people are drawn to the tales we tell connecting people and things. We are innately attuned to these kinds of messages. Stories work.

If I were to ask you to tell me the story of the product you are trying to sell, how would you respond? It might be the history of it, but I suspect that you'd be able to show your passion for your product more effectively if you can tie it to things that represent value and are memorable. For some reason, people have an easier time remembering things with stories attached to them. If you want to be memorable, to reach people on an emotional level, to engage them, to be memorable, and to show them how you can be of service and of value to them, package your message as a story.

# INFO OVERLOAD

The biggest change I have seen in our profession of sales is the proliferation of information. You can Google the latest research on how much time the average American spends on technology and the boundless source of information that is at all of our fingertips. For many in sales, and for our customers, this can lead to information overload which is defined as "stress induced by reception of more information than is necessary to make a decision (or that can be understood and digested in the time available)." Ouch! We all know salespeople who think it's a good strategy to pile on fact after fact about a product or service only to receive a blank stare in the prospect's eyes from the stress of information overload.

The antidote is to look at data in a different way. Allow me to provide an illustration. Have you heard of Howard Moskowitz? He's a market researcher and psychophysicist best known for his approach to information related to spaghetti sauce. In the 1970s, Moskowitz was commissioned by Pepsi to find the perfect taste that would appeal to the largest number of consumers. The data from his research was scattered all over the place with no singular preference emerging. His conclusion was that there was no one, preferred taste—there were, for example, many perfect levels of sweetness depending on the audience. In 1986, there was a battle between two spaghetti sauce manufacturers, Prego and Ragu.

Although Prego was thicker than Ragu, with diced tomatoes vs puree, Prego was in a slump. Instead of standard practice—asking a focus group of spaghetti eaters what they wanted—Howard Moskowitz worked with Campbell's kitchens to come up with 45 varieties of sauce, differing in spiciness, sweetness, tartness, saltiness, thickness, aroma, mouth feel, cost, etc. Then he took it on the road and asked focus groups of people to eat and rate them, discovering that everyone had a slightly different definition of the perfect sauce. It was not his goal to create 45 new sauces for sale. He wondered whether there was an opportunity to find a new product. They found one group that was totally untapped—those who liked their sauce with lots of ingredients in it. Extra chunky sauce launched in 1989, and it proved to be worth hundreds of millions of dollars. There is no one right version of a dish. The solution came after the gathering of data.

People sometimes ask me what is the single biggest change in the sales industry since I started decades ago. That's an easy one. The fundamentals haven't changed at all. We are still in the business of forming relationships. Our goals are to help customers and to do it by out-performing the competition. Still, the largest shift in the way we do business is this: information.

Years ago, if you went to a customer and had a lot of data about a product, a trend, or about what their competitors are doing, you would have been seen as a genius. Today, that kind of knowledge is merely the baseline of competence. It is assumed that everyone has access to almost unlimited amounts of information because it is so readily available online. That's not bad news. It presents us an opportunity to differentiate ourselves. Let me explain.

You are brimming with ideas and information, almost too much of it, but think of your customer. All of this data flying at them is overwhelming. You can prove yourself invaluable to a customer in the way you manage that tidal wave of information. You can be their protection against overload. Here's how.

Serve as a filter. It's your job to know everything you can about your product and your customer's business. It's not your job to say it out loud. Customers are burdened with too much data as it is. Keep them up to date, present new ideas to them logically, and help them get past all the noise in order to find the ideas that matter most to them.

Be relevant. You will be most useful to customers when you can repackage all of the data out there and tailor it to their specific goals. The question to continually ask yourself before you do a verbal data-dump is, "Why will this matter to them?" If you can't answer it concretely, you're not helping.

Let "the new" sink in. You should acknowledge that it takes some time for new products, techniques, and services to be accepted by the customer. Give customers some room to breathe and to consider the ramifications of ideas you present to them that are new. However great the next big thing sounds to you, a customer has to process it carefully and consider its consequences. Help them organize thoughts. Finally, don't take their indecision as a rejection. Circle back later and see whether they have warmed up to the new.

Know everything. Easier said than done, I know. The customer may be overwhelmed with information, but that doesn't let you off the hook. If anything, it is an additional burden upon every good salesperson to invest even more time to stay current. In order to keep ahead of the competition, you have to be smarter and faster too. Especially when the information is time-sensitive, you simply have to be first.

# NEW CUSTOMER CALLS

Even if prepared with impactful questions and a story that sells, every salesperson in the world gets nervous when calling on a new customer. That's perfectly normal. (It means you're alive.) We all need a little stress to motivate us to excel. You can channel that stress, calm fears and relieve anxieties by preparing beforehand.

Keeping focused, calm, and being positive helps. Here are a few tips to get your mind into the game and to keep your nerves out of it.

Obviously, you start with a positive outlook. (There's more about having a positive attitude, or what I call food-itude, in the next chapter.) But there are additional techniques that I've found helpful. Call—and by call I mean visit—at a time of day that is most likely to be ideal. You might not know exactly when that is since you don't know the person yet, but use some common sense. Don't call on someone when they are most likely to be busy, exhausted, or otherwise distracted. These considerations might be industry-specific or more general. They refer to times of day and also times of the year. For example, don't call on an accountant during tax time, right? Don't call on a restaurant during lunch rush. You get the idea. It's common sense, but you'd be surprised how often salespeople set themselves up for failure because they don't take schedules into consideration.

I like to begin conversations with a sincere compliment about their business. Then you might say that you'd love to be a partner in their success. Keep the conversation breezy and without pressure, and you can express your interest in the customer faster than you might imagine. When you focus on the customer, it takes some of the pressure off of you. Instead of worrying what you'll say and how you'll perform, asking valuable questions, actively listening, and talking about the customer is easier and will be welcomed more readily.

Psych yourself up for the call before you begin. You'll be able to maintain a more positive attitude (which in turn will help you focus and keep you from giving up too soon) if you can remember past experiences of success in similar situations. Deep breathing and visualizing success can help build positive physical and mental energy.

A friendly tone of voice is both comforting to you and reassuring to the customer. It is the same as if you were meeting someone in a social setting. You want people to want to get to know you and like you. Be enthusiastic and keep the sound of your voice relaxed.

And smile.

You probably are not nervous talking to your friends, so as quickly as you can, think of the customer as a friend. Dale Carnegie, the self-improvement pioneer, said that "a person's name is to that person the sweetest and most important sound in any language." It's true. How do you feel when someone calls you by your name in a friendly and genuine manner? I like to use a customer's name within the first five seconds of the call. And I continue to use their name throughout our conversation. That technique is great for the customer because everyone likes to be referred to by name, but it is also helpful to you and will keep the nerves calm.

As you talk, keep your antennae up. What I mean is that you need to be aware of how the potential customer is responding to you. To a great extent, he or she will provide a roadmap of how to proceed. While it's true that there might be occasional roadblocks, there are ways to be persuasive and move toward a common goal. If you think about the conversation as a map, you can more easily strategize where you need to turn next. You won't feel quite as lost, and that's good too.

Finally, after the conversation is done, replay it in your head to decipher what happened and what should happen next. Sometimes, as you contemplate it, you'll realize that there might have been opportunities and cues that you missed at the time. You might discover that you can take a different approach with the same person and remedy or improve the situation after stepping away from it and looking at it objectively. At the very least, you'll be able to improve your performance, and the outcome, next time.

# REFERRALS

The prospect has become a customer and then a repeat customer as your partnership and relationship grows. A logical step somewhere along the way is to secure one of the most valuable wins in the sales universe—a referral. Before I share some ideas on how and when to earn this advantage, let me share some information about how natural it is to network.

I was reading the other day about how traditional Native American gardening techniques are so successful. One technique is called "companion planting" and it is tailored to get the highest yields possible from three symbiotic plants—beans, corn, and squash. Beans are planted next to corn, whose stalks are perfect for the climbing vines of the bean plants. In turn, the beans roots capture nitrogen from the air, and enrich the soil which is ideal for the corn. The squash is planted in between rows of corn and beans, with its large leaves acting as a ground cover, keeping the weeds away, providing shade for the corn's roots, and keeping the ground moist to help the beans grow. When this tradition started, Native Americans believed the "three sisters" were magical when grown together, and that they should also be eaten together. They also believed that since they protected each other while growing, they would protect whoever ate them together. Early European settlers were given the gift of the three sisters by Native Americans which ties to the story behind our Thanksgiving celebration.

Back to referrals. Here's a quiz for you. Who is your most powerful source of new business? Is it a sales team member with boundless energy or the old pro who's been at the sales game forever? Maybe it's the boss who is great at motivating you or the office staff that provides terrific support. However good those folks are, they're not as helpful to you as someone who's not on the company payroll: your current customers.

A loyal customer is a gift that keeps on giving. Yes, they regularly supply you with orders (thank you!) but there is something potentially more valuable than that. Much more valuable. A loyal customer is your best shot at free advertising. Every time they talk to other people, they can potentially talk about you. And if you receive good word of mouth, half of your job is already done. Particularly with referrals, loyal customers generate the kind of leads that money can't buy.

I suggest four ways to mine customer referrals for sales gold:

- The first step to receiving referrals is to prove yourself worthy of getting them. That's accomplished when you serve the customers perfectly. Invoice accurately, provide top-notch communication and superior service. Go the extra mile. Sometimes there will be gaps and hiccups. Use those experiences as opportunities to prove yourself. If you can turn potentially negative experiences to continued validation of your proactive thinking on your customer's behalf, you're halfway home. Prove yourself.

- In order to receive, first you have to give. This principle is especially true with business to business sales. I sometimes will prime the pump to get referrals. I will go to a business customer and refer them to my friends. Then I report on that to the customers. I said, "Hey, I think you're great. I told my best friends about you and they're going to be your customers too." If you've built up a good relationship, the customer will then return the favor and refer you to others. You might even ask directly, "Do you know other people who could benefit from my products and services?" This give and take only works if you are sincere and do your part first.

- The best of all possible scenarios is when the customer goes even farther than giving you a referral and makes a direct introduction. This could be over lunch or a conference call. A testimonial like this is invaluable. After meeting the customer's referral, it is imperative that you engage the prospect carefully and respectfully. In a sense, you are managing two relationships in one. Be sure to properly acknowledge to your customer your gratitude for the introduction.

- Using the advantage of referrals can be a challenge. I find that, as in most effective stages of sales and life, preparedness is paramount. Sometimes, these referrals will come out of the blue. You'll be talking to a customer or you'll pick up the phone and there will be a golden opportunity, given to you on a silver tray by a customer. The way that you respond will determine whether you seal the deal or crash and burn. In your mind, prepare in advance various responses to referrals that highlight your commitment to the customer and your promise that you will treat the referral (who is likely a friend of the customer) with your full attention. If you can make the experience even more profitable for the customer doing the referral, the likelihood is that the referrals will keep on coming.

And that is where the tie to the Native American's proven technique of the three sisters comes in. When referrals start flowing and growing, they reinforce themselves creating "win-win-win" situations for you, your original customer, and the referral. The result can be a bountiful crop of sales.

# ROCKY TIMES

Popcorn saved the movie theatres during the Depression by providing a new revenue stream with a huge profit margin of 75%. Popcorn made the difference between whether a theatre would survive or not at the time. Other Depression era successes include the King Kullen grocery store chain, selling more than 1,000 basic food products at a lower cost than local shops, and Carl Swanson's frozen turkey business. Swanson worked out a win-win solution by guaranteeing struggling farmers in February that he would purchase their turkeys in the fall, and advanced funds in the spring to help pay for feed. By 1942 he became the nation's largest turkey processor, leading to even greater success in the 1950s with his Swanson's TV dinners.

When times are good, a certain euphoria fills the air. People open their wallets. Their confidence lifts all boats. Sales professionals find good times are a good time to be in the business. It won't come as shocking news to read that prosperous times don't last forever. I think of that as good news, frankly. Challenging periods in the business cycle are opportunities for you to distinguish yourself.

When times get tough, the landscape changes. Weak players get shaken out. There is consolidation. Customers who are well prepared look at a down-market as a time to regroup, to strategize, and when the time is right, to grab market share away from competitors. As a salesperson, you can do the same thing.

Downturns are not business as usual. In sales, the way we sell needs to shift when money's tight. For one thing, it's stressful and people are gloomy. That's an opportunity for you. People want to be around others who can lift their spirits. You can take it too far, of course, but try to maintain an upbeat attitude. In your conversations, keep the big picture in mind. This will help your customers see through the emotional fog.

You will need to be empathetic too, as customers face serious trials. This refers to a general attitude of compassion, but it is more than that. Arm yourself with information about the current situation of your customers. Walk in their shoes a little. This experience will give you insight into ways to best help them. Determine what are the biggest challenges that they face and then look at your list of products and services as potential remedies. When you present them with your findings, discuss the options as solutions.

When money is tight, value is king. Every thought has to revolve around the concepts of preserving financial stability, improvements that add to the bottom line, and savings. This doesn't mean, necessarily, that your best products and services in this environment are the cheapest, but it does highlight the emphasis that must be placed on value and strategic advantage.

If you can help a customer get through rough days, they will be loyal forever. It is not a time to pull back and lower your expectations. Challenging economies require a shift on your part to be sensitive to any opportunities that create or conserve value. As the economy improves, the message changes to taking advantage of new opportunities. In sales our message has to continually shift and react to the real-world landscape of our customers.

# IT'S ABOUT TIME

Time is money. I've found that to be true over my career. But I'm not talking about your time. It's valuable too, I guess, but if you really want to focus on value, find your customer some extra time. If you can provide services and products that will make your customer more efficient, able to work smarter, or to enjoy more free time, you have a winning combination. I can think of three ways to achieve that aim: questions, investigations, and sharing.

You already know the virtues of the thing you're selling. You know how it operates and what it can do for others. What you might not know is how the customer can use it to save time. So ask. Try to determine the ways the customer can streamline energies and become more profitable by using the thing you're offering to save time. Ask direct questions following the guidelines we outlined earlier: "When do you feel the most time-constrained? What are the scheduling bottlenecks? What happens when you get overwhelmed?"

Next, research solutions specific to the customer's needs. Do the legwork necessary to discover how his or her competitors are managing time issues. If you can, investigate emerging technologies, techniques, and studies that can give your customer an advantage. This line of thinking is not limited to business sales. Commercial customers value their time, but retail customers are also looking for ways to maximize their time. They might not put a price tag on it as if they were in an office, but if you can provide someone with a way to have an extra chunk of leisure time, that's golden too.

Lastly, share the information with customers in a way that they can appreciate what the idea will mean to their schedule. When you think about it from the point of view of a clock, it's easier to persuade someone that the precious resource of time has added value. It is all well and good to say, "Here's the newest thing." However, if you can prove that this new thing can make their life work more smoothly, faster, better, smarter, you'll be onto something significant in terms of the customer experience.

# SECRET SAUCE

Let's review the main points of this chapter:

Think of explaining yourself as telling a story, to make it memorable.

Seek to know everything, including when *not* to tell everything you know.

One way you can add value to a customer is to be their info filter.

Make your first conversation great and then analyze it.

The perfect formula is to create loyalty, which encourages referrals, ultimately
    creating new customers, and then the cycle repeats.

Bad economic times can be good news if you're prepared.

Customers want to save money, and they want to save time, too.

In this chapter, much of the discussion centered on communication. But to truly excel at it, any communicator has to get creative. Why is that? Because with the constant din of information, business-as-usual blather gets lost entirely. It requires extra effort and planning to be good at telling a story in an engaging way, but if you're not memorable, why bother? It is worth the time to plan and organize your communications and to put some kind of creative spin on it in order to break through the wall many people build as protection against information overload.

Of course, it is logical to be wary of anything that takes time away from making a sale, but if you work smart, these hours spent are worth it. As customers give you free advertising in the form of referrals, as they stay with you as competitors knock on their doors, as you have a financial backstop in rocky times: all of these are consequences of establishing a great relationship, and that is cemented with communication. It takes some time, but don't forget that it will save time in the long run.

# INGREDIENT 4
## EXUDE FOOD-ITUDE

The only real stumbling block is fear of failure. In cooking, you have to have a what-the-hell attitude.
Julia Child, The French Chef

In March of 1917, a few weeks before the United States entered World War I, Charles Lathrop Pack, one of America's wealthiest men, formed the National War Garden Commission. His fortune came from his family's timber business. He foresaw the need to bolster home gardening. The world's farms were being devastated as soldiers left home to fight. In 1914 in France, three million farmers left their fields; in Russia, eight million. Nations called upon all men of fighting age to shoulder a rifle throughout Europe. The majority of soldiers listed their vocation as: farmer. This meant that suddenly, a continent's farms were stripped of male labor. Pack's goal in America was to compensate for the looming loss in agriculture giving home gardeners a sense of pride and productivity. A campaign was launched to encourage private and public lands to be used to grow food for families. This resulted in five million gardens by the end of the war.

During World War II, the Victory Garden reappeared as an important source of psychological and practical comfort. In the U.S., twenty million Americans planted gardens both at home and in public spaces. It is estimated that 40 percent of all the produce consumed during the war came from victory gardens. Many homes enjoyed a common dish made from these vegetables into a soup. It became known as Victory Garden Soup.

It was a perfect combination for difficult times. Is there anything more comforting than soup—nutritious, nurturing, warm, healing. Even today, every culture in the world values the restorative and healing properties of soup. Miss Manners once wrote, "Do you have a kinder, more adaptable friend in the food world than soup?"

In this chapter, I want to talk about the qualities in sales that are warm and generous—the professional equivalents of soup. I call it food-itude, the nurturing and comforting qualities we understand from the fields of nutrition and psychology but relating to the business of sales. What are the attributes that make someone think of you as a kind, adaptable friend? And how do you develop the skills that give people a warm feeling inside after their business dealings with you? These are food-itudes. Let's dig in.

# WARMTH

In making a sale, there is technique, intelligence, and skill, but there is also another ingredient involved that is harder to quantify. This X factor is often the difference between success and failure. I am no better at describing it than writers through the ages who have struggled to understand the mysterious attraction between people. I do know that when people feel some kind of connection, the transactions between them—whether personal or business—are smooth and effortless.

I came across an analogy that I like in a book by the contemporary restaurateur Danny Meyer, who owns a booming portfolio of eateries that range from four-star distinction to burger and fries excellence. As Meyer describes his hunt for an ideal employee who is capable of giving 100 percent for the benefit of the customer, he describes a moth drawn to a light bulb. Forty-nine percent of the moth's motivation is for the brightness of the bulb. The light is what attracts it. But the larger stake, 51 percent, is the warmth of the light source. The moth responds to warmth. This is why it stays close to the bulb.

People are the same. However tough and cynical we may appear, we react to warmth. I see this as a core emotional need. Meyer lists five skills that he looks for in his recruitment. I think the same translate perfectly in broader sales.

Optimism. Sales professionals require a sense that anything is possible. They achieve their goals, not by ruthlessness, but by acknowledging the needs of customers which include showing them kindness and thoughtfulness. They see the glass half full and have a positive vision of the future and what is possible.

Learning. We've touched on this in the first chapter and several times since. Those who are best in sales are insatiably curious. Their goal is access to new ways of seeing the world through understanding the gathering of intelligence. And then transforming that intelligence into information and value for the customer.

Love of work. Salespeople cultivate a desire to accomplish a task the best that it can be. They are not afraid of labor; rather they find satisfaction in accomplishing things that they previously thought impossible.

Caring. The most successful salespeople have unique abilities to feel empathy for others. Their awareness of the needs of customers gives them special insight to serve them. This is almost intuitive, but it can be learned.

Self-knowledge. People who thrive in a sales environment are students of human behavior. They want to know what makes people tick, and they begin their investigation into the human condition by turning inward. They are self-aware, honest, and accountable.

# GRATITUDE IS AN ATTITUDE

Most of us are good at showing appreciation…at least once a year on Thanksgiving Day. For the rest of the year, well, many of us could use some help.

George Neumann was my first branch manager. He told us every time we gathered for a sales meeting that we needed to be grateful for our customers. He drilled into us the value of acknowledging how important their business was to us, and he expected us to thank them on every single business call. The message got through to me. I have always practiced the habit of showing gratitude to customers. This practice has altered the way I do business, and I recommend it highly to you.

If you need a little help to get things started, I suggest that you take a little time and write down your customers' names. Alongside that list, note at least one thing that you wish to thank each one of them for giving to you. This will become an action checklist. Take this list of personalized thanks and make appointments with each customer to thank them individually for the relationship you've built together.

I will make you a guarantee. If you do this, for one thing, you'll get better at it. More importantly, your customers will be surprised and they will see you in a different light afterwards. They will remember you as a person rather than as a product's conduit. If you can present your gratitude in a way that is sincere and direct, you'll solidify and strengthen your working relationship. You'll find more joy in your work, you'll be more easily energized, and you'll prosper.

# RECOGNITION

I heard about two Purdue University students named Brett and Cameron who walked around campus each day and passed out recognition to students. They were following the advice of Abraham Lincoln who noted, "Everybody likes a compliment." The idea began during the economic downturn. The boys thought that free recognition would be a way to cheer up a gloomy student body who were feeling the change of atmosphere on campus. They were also going for a more personal transformation, and they reported that students would respond, "It makes my day." Soon, their efforts grabbed the attention of national news and entertainment broadcasts. They took their recognition program to other cities on a multi-city tour.

Genuine rcognition has staying power. A recent study shows that when recognition is given in the right spirit, the impact it has on the recipient can last up to a week. The byproducts of recognition include an increase in productivity, feelings of positivity, and openness. As a sales tool, a well-delivered statement of recognition can be effective and lasting.

Review the following guides to more effective recognition.

- There is a difference between genuine recognition and flattery. The old saying, "flattery will get you nowhere" holds true. People can see through a false comment, and it will be counterproductive in sales because it makes the customer uneasy and suspicious of your intentions. On the other hand, genuine recognition increases your chances of sales success.

- Recognition should be specific and avoid being too personal. When you recognize someone, they will feel more accepting if it is a specific action. Sales people who are the most successful using recognition stay clear of comments that are inappropriate. "Your business looks great" is much better than "your hair looks great."

- Recognition reinforces good behavior. When someone hears a positive comment, it feels good and they want to experience that feeling again. As a result, they will act in ways that earn additional recognition. Understand this basic human reaction and use recognition to guide customers to behaviors that are sales-conducive.

- Testing. Recognition needs to ring true. If you're not sure whether it will sound hollow or not, try it out with friends first. Use an observation about something you admire and see how friends react. Don't forget to smile.

- Give and take. If it is an art to give genuine recognition, it is also an art to be a gracious recipient. Your first impulse might be to shrug it off. It even feels modest to do so. But you will never learn to excel at the give and take of recognition without being comfortable on both sides of it. Accept recognition with sincere thanks.

# YOU NEED LAUGHTER

An American journalist wrote, "Men need laughter sometimes more than food." I need both, and I'm unwilling to live without either. In sales, humor is a terrific business aid. It's a must-have skill. Work life is stressful for most of us. I think of laughter as the way we manage to get through the day. It makes us more productive because it helps us to keep going when we would otherwise slow down and give up. The comedian Milton Berle once said, "Laughter is an instant vacation."

There is a rejuvenating power about a good, strong, gut-busting, laugh. Dr. Wayne Dyer wrote, "It's impossible for you to be angry and laugh at the same time." True, and furthermore, laughter helps us get over being angry. Jay Leno noted, "You cannot be mad at somebody who makes you laugh—it's as simple as that." I find that laughter is a perfect way to solidify relationships. It makes me feel relaxed and optimistic. When I share a laugh with a customer, it forges a bond.

The rise of the celebrity chef—the key is humor, as evidenced by some of the best by the late Anthony Bourdain in his book, *Kitchen Confidential: Adventures in the Culinary Underbelly*: "Your body is not a temple, it's an amusement park. Enjoy the ride." And, "A proper saute pan, for instance, should cause serious head injury if brought down hard against someone's skull. If you have any doubts about which will dent — the victim's head or your pan — then throw that pan right in the trash."

Here are some qualities about laughter that you may not have considered:

- Laughter improves morale.
- Laughter helps people cope with problems.
- Laughter leads to creativity.
- Laughing makes you more alert.
- Laughter leads to teamwork.

- Laughter eases stress.
- Laughing people are more motivated.
- Laughter removes barriers.
- Laughter makes people feel less judgmental.
- Laughter makes you memorable.
- Laughter is healthy for your mind and body.

You don't have to feel like you are a comedian to be good at generating laughter. Solicit humor in your conversations with customers. Ask, "What's the funniest thing that happened to you today?"

# BUILDING ON MOMENTUM

Every once in a while, I'll have a perfect day. You've probably experienced the same thing. It's as if you can do no wrong. Everywhere you look, you find success. Everything goes right, almost in spite of you. These are good days. I don't know why they happen, but I'm glad they occasionally do happen.

I've noticed, in the middle of days like these, that I find myself re-energized. I am full of a newfound enthusiasm for living and working. The Greek word *entheos* is the root of enthusiasm; it means full of spirit. When everything is going well, this fullness of spirit builds. It is a cumulative wave that propels me to do more than I imagined was possible.

If you are lucky enough to have such a day, take full advantage of it. Call on customers, make contact with as many people as you can, and share your enthusiasm with them. There is a reason why enthusiasm is self-perpetuating. When everything is going well, we radiate a different level of confidence. Customers can sense that energy and they will respond to it. A change comes over us. It is a springier step, a wider smile, a shift in our tone of voice. In these moments, our customers see us differently. We are shown in our most positive light.

When you are in the groove, do whatever you can to ride the wave of enthusiasm. Success begets success. You will be more likely to engage customers in such moments. It is tempting to celebrate your successes when all's going so well. But don't. Use the positive energy to make even more of it. There will be time for kicking back and celebrating later (these kinds of days don't last forever, after all); you can celebrate then.

Enthusiasm and the momentum that is naturally attached to it is slightly mysterious, but you are the one making it happen. You energize your customers, you take your talents and skills and parlay them into positive results, and you channel that fullness of spirit to make great things happen. And there is an additional aspect of this good energy: you give portions of it to everyone you meet.

# THE INNER YOU

You are what you eat. Well, maybe. But I came across a quotation by Zig Zigglar, the sales guru, a few years ago that I think fits even better, "You are who you are and what you are because of what has gone into your mind. You can change who you are and what you are—by changing what goes into your mind." I like this point of view. I find it empowering.

A colleague told a story that has always remained with me. It seems that once there lived a man who made his living selling hot dogs on the side of the road. He was an old man, hard of hearing and dim-sighted. He didn't read a newspaper. He didn't own a radio. He had a simple life: he went to the street and sold hot dogs, very good hot dogs, and he made a nice living. Over time, his business grew. Everyone liked his hot dogs, and he had a loyal clientele.

One day, his son came home from college to help in the family business. He said to his father, "Dad, what are you doing? Haven't you heard on the radio that there is a terrible Depression?"

The father thought to himself, "My son is smarter than I am. He's been to college, he reads the newspapers and listens to radio reports. Surely he knows what he's saying."

The old man shut down most of his operations. He no longer stood on the roadside, and he ordered less food for sale. Immediately, sales plummeted. He went to his son and said, "You were right son. We are in a terrible Depression. We have no business."

This little fable is extreme, but I commonly run across people who are filling their minds with ideas that are no less damaging. It is a dangerous thing to convince ourselves that we are bound to fail. It is never true. Sales professionals are adaptive, creative, enterprising, and determined. From time to time, negative messages will sneak into your mind. I suggest that you fill your thoughts instead with ideas that encourage rather than discourage. Crowd negative messages out of your head completely.

# SECRET SAUCE

Let's review the main points of this chapter:

The X-factor in a sale is often an interpersonal connection.
Positivity and showing gratitude for it often leads to more of both.
Sincere recognition, unlike hollow flattery, draw people to you.
Laughter, as it turns out, really is the best medicine...for sales.
A powerful energy is the momentum of success itself.
Positive mental attitutdes build a career while negative ones can destroy it.

It is sometimes difficult to quantify the virtues of positivity and mental attitudes, and yet these intangibles often make the difference between success and failure in sales. When trying to describe a category of these concepts, I hit upon "food-itude" because the word suggested to me the emotional comfort and warmth that food provides as well as the physical fuel that the body needs. In sales, there is a necessary attitude of warmth, gratitude, humor, and positivity that is every bit as important to life in the business as food is to life itself.

While it is true that some people seem to be innately gifted with food-itude, I believe that each of us can amp up those levels by developing techniques that are responsive to our customers' emotional needs.

# INGREDIENT 5
## COMMAND CONFIDENCE

In the summer of 1519, Hernan Cortes led some 500 men to the Aztec capital city of Tenochtitlan. Cortes had spent the previous fifteen years in and around Hispaniola and Cuba, and the trip into Mexico was to be a strategic voyage to claim Mexico for the king of Spain. He was greeted by Moctezuma II and invited into his palace as a guest. The palace was a splendid series of large buildings. For example, there were two zoos, an aquarium with ten ponds for salt water and ten ponds for fresh water, and a magnificent botanical garden.

In the garden, Cortes saw a strange plant with red fruit. He harvested seeds from it and sent them to Europe. One of the unique features of the garden was a collection of plants to be used for medicinal purposes, an unusual practice in the eyes of the Europeans. The red fruited plant was thought to be medicinal. They were tomatoes.

The plants "discovered" by Cortes were eyed suspiciously in the Old World. Europeans planted tomatoes as ornaments in a garden, not to produce food; furthermore, they were thought to have hallucinatory powers. An Italian herbalist in the mid-16th century called them "dangerous and harmful." It was thought that even the smell of them could cause headaches and eye diseases. The negative reputation stuck.

In fact, it took 150 more years for people to rid themselves of their dark opinions of tomatoes and to use them in cooking. Thomas Jefferson was one of the first North Americans to plant tomatoes. In his garden, he records having planted and eaten them beginning in 1809. Finally, in 1897, Joseph Campbell created and sold condensed tomato soup, and the redemption of the plant from the Aztecs was complete.

Sales professionals also have to be mindful of our reputation. In order to be successful, we have to know what our customers and potential customers think of us. Sometimes it will require boldness, even courage, when others are relying on incorrect information—tomatoes are not poisonous—or misperceptions about you. Command confidence. In this chapter, I present tips about sales from the perspective of the customer: How do they view you? Why should they trust you? How can you be the kind of person who encourages loyalty?

# "I'VE NEVER HEARD OF YOU"

It is one thing to sell a product that everyone already knows, or a product from a company everyone knows. A lot of the initial work is already done for you. A salesperson for Coca-Cola, for example, doesn't really have to go into great detail about what the beverage tastes like. The brand has made an introduction for you. The task of selling something unfamiliar is trickier.

And yet, I would argue, every sales conversation must cover the same basic material because a customer has to feel confident about you and your product. It's more than that, however; sales are transactions of trust. You can't trust someone you don't know. How do you tell your sales story to inspire trust?

First, discover whether they want to hear more. Ask questions as you talk to gauge their interest. Try to observe whether they are uncomfortable, rushed, bored, or preoccupied, and if so, determine whether you should continue, take a different approach, or reschedule. They may not want to hear more, but is that because they haven't heard what they need to hear or is it something more fundamental?

Next, ask yourself why it should matter to them. This question of relevance is critical. If you have done your homework in advance, you should know already why your products or services are a good fit for the prospective customer. The bigger question is how can you find an approach that makes your goals and the customer's needs align? You need to find some common ground, something about yourself and your product that they can relate to. I've found that the best way to do this is by telling stories.

Tell your tale. I'm not thinking of fiction here. Tell your prospective customers about yourself, your product, where it came from, how it's affected others, and so forth. These are the stories that connect people. Most importantly, the stories have to be believable. If people believe you, they will listen to you and follow you.

Finally, be sincere. Decisions to buy things are emotional choices. Some surveys have suggested that as many as 80 percent of purchase decisions are emotionally connected. They will buy from you if they can trust you, if they are convinced you will care about them and give them good service. These feelings are generated when they hear your story and (because it's sincere) they believe it.

It is a short distance from "I've never heard of you" to "I like what you're about." The gap between the two must be traveled, and for many people, it can be a quick trip…if you know how to do it.

# WHY BUY IT?

Put yourself in your customers' shoes for a moment. Why do you buy things? Or more specifically, why do you buy what you buy? You have choices, after all. There are very few monopolies in the world of business. So ask yourself what makes the difference between the options you have.

Off the top of my head, I can think of a half dozen motivators in sales. Every product doesn't satisfy the needs of every individual, but as a group, the following represent the reasons why people buy.

- It's new. Products and services that are new create their own, special kind of momentum. People are curious and optimistic, and these traits translate into a belief that new products are innovative and somehow better, and discovering them satisfies their curiosity.
- It makes me feel safe. The basic human need to feel protected often translates into sales. When people are anxious, they look for things that can help them. We sell those things. The action of a sale itself is all about reassurance. We communicate these values to people as we describe what our product can do for them. In business relationships, feeling safe means being profitable.

- It's easy. People are constantly looking for ways to make their lives more convenient. Businesses want to streamline and be more efficient. In both cases, the products that can, in some way, provide solutions to the ever-present issues of being overwhelmed have powerful advantages.
- It's cool. A sale is something like being granted entrance into an exclusive club. Owning something desirable grants status. This is as true for a sale of a multi-million dollar object to a cool new toy that sells for $1, but that every kid wants. The affiliation with something of value is, itself, a value.
- It makes me better. People and businesses are perpetually looking for ways to improve. They want to amplify what they already have with something that sets them apart and makes them better, smarter, faster, leaner, stronger, more....
- It will help me win. This motivator is simple. We all want to win, and we are drawn to products and services that give us an edge.

Customers are motivated differently and moreover, their motivations change over time. Sales professionals who truly excel are those who can tap into the motivations of their customers and can respond to them instinctively.

# SALES AND FRIENDS

I have two stories that illustrate the power of friendship in business. The first is using the environment of a friend as a model, and the second is the example of friendship as a connecting point in a transaction.

Fun facts: the word "companion" is Latin for someone with whom you share bread. The word "restaurant" is from the French verb *restaurer*, meaning to restore.

The history of the word "restaurant" is pretty interesting. It dates back from Paris in 1782, where it was coined by a Parisian gastronome named Antoine Beauvilliers. He opened the Grand Taverne de Londres in the French capital with a chef poached from the aristocracy and a menu that allowed customers to choose what they wanted to eat. Brillat-Savarin said the restaurant was "the first to combine the four essentials of an elegant room, smart waiters, a choice cellar and superior cooking." Beauvilliers remembered his customers' names and tastes, walked them through the menu and made suggestions for dishes they might enjoy.

And consider this story about Abraham Lincoln. When he first set his sights on a life of public service in politics, people were skeptical of him. He had no business experience, and on paper it didn't seem like he was capable of much. Looking back after his presidency, people said this about his initial prospects: "Lincoln had nothing, only plenty of friends."

I like that quotation about Lincoln because I believe that friendship has unlimited power. In sales, it is an important part of success. If people have a choice between two options, and if the two are roughly the same, they will opt for the thing offered by a friend. They will choose the friend every time. All things being equal, friends buy from friends. All things being not as equal, they will still buy from friends.

Skeptical salespeople will argue, "Well, I can't be a friend to everyone." Let me say for the record, yes you can. You can befriend everyone you meet. The qualities of friendship—the trust, the service, the loyalty and the intimacy—can be demonstrated as you sell. What's more, they must be demonstrated.

- You show trustworthiness by proving that you are as good as your word.
- You prove your capacity for service when you go beyond the expected.
- You become a partner with your customers when you anticipate their needs.

- You demonstrate your friendship when you put their interests ahead of your own.

# FAIR-WEATHER FRIENDSHIP

It's easy to be a friend when times are good. People tend to show their true colors, unfortunately, when things get tough. I've found this in my personal life, but also in business. Everyone wants to be with a winner. With a loser, not as much.

But there is an interesting flipside to this human trait. And sales professionals can show their expertise by paying attention to the psychology of bad times. In a crisis, people feel vulnerable. They circle the wagons, they batten down the hatches. This can be good news for you. When a catastrophe looms, people need trusted advisers. They want to gather around them others with expertise who have been through a disaster before and have weathered the storm. Trust is a prerequisite.

The following are some ideas for strengthening loyalty in preparation for your customers' challenges:

- Focus on value and be aware of the customer's fears about pricing.
- Know everything there is to know about your product so customers will trust your expertise.
- If you want customers to be loyal to you, be an advocate and be loyal to them.
- In every interaction with customers, be sincere.
- When customers are frightened, frustrated, or anxious, take time to listen.

# TOMBSTONE INTEGRITY

When I die—and I'm in no hurry for that day—I want it to be said that I was a man of integrity. To me, that word is even more powerful than wealth, power, influence, or reputation. I don't know what they'll carve on my tombstone, but I want to be known as a person who cared about what I said, what I did, and more than that, that I did what I said.

Here's a question for you. If someone were to ask you to grade yourself on this statement, what letter grade A-F would you earn?

My word is golden. When I say I will do something, it gets done.

Do you always keep your word? Most of the time? Sometimes? When you have to?

It's not a moralistic question when it comes to business. Customers respond to the belief that you can be trusted. Let's face it, the knock on our profession is that we're a bunch of shady characters who will try to pull the wool over customers' eyes for a quick buck. I can't deny that I've met a few people in sales like that, but there's not a place for that behavior any longer in our profession. Reputation matters, and furthermore, it travels with you in an unshakeable way. In the age of Facebook and anonymous postings of customer service feedback, you must maintain a 100 percent honesty mantra.

Whatever you say you will do, it has to happen. Therefore, think before you promise something. Next, when you do commit to something, communicate its parameters clearly. Document what you've agreed to do. And lastly and most obviously, get it done.

# MORE THAN LOYAL

Recently, I read a study about customers who rated their experience with sales professionals as satisfied or very satisfied. The study was developed to understand how customer satisfaction translated into loyalty to a brand. The results were a bit strange. Most people didn't express strong feelings one way or the other when they were satisfied—there's not a lot of difference between being satisfied and very satisfied. At least, that's not the main distinction that will cause them to become loyal customers. Simply being satisfied isn't enough. Even being very satisfied is not enough.

What is it then that makes the difference? Customers who self-identify as "loyal" note that they feel an emotional connection to the brand or to the sales person. That's an interesting distinction, isn't it?

We have all tried for years to be satisfaction-sensitive in our work. In sales, we want to make sure the customer is happy, but this study points to something deeper and more personal.

For me, one of the triggers for an emotional connection is a sense of engagement. As a sales professional, how would you rate yourself? Respond to the following statements.

- I am passionate about my work and I continuously attempt to make a strong connection with people regarding products and services.
- I work hard and I put in my time, but there's a big chunk of my day that is coasting along.
- I find myself being unhappy more frequently than happy. I tend to complain a lot, and I'm not as productive as I probably should be.

Back to the customers, they respond emotionally to you and your level of engagement. That's the thing about passion—it rubs off on people.

# THE MYSTERY OF CONFIDENCE

What is self-confidence? Is it like your bank account and as you make deposits of successes your ledger grows in strength until you feel like you have enough emotional capital to achieve anything? Or is confidence a genetic trait that some people seem to have from the start—the folks who are good at everything they try, or if not, they instinctively know how to find help to become better? Should we look at self-confidence more cynically than that? Maybe it is like a coat we put on to protect ourselves from fears and dangers. Even when we are not confident, we can fake it with a costume of impenetrability.

I thought of each of these three possibilities recently as I watched a student violin recital. There is nothing quite like the sound of children sawing away on miniature string instruments, is there? Anyway, as I watched each student slowly take the performer's position in front of the group of parents and their teacher, I noticed that some of them gave off an air of complete control. It was as if they either were unaware that there was any pressure on them, or they had such poise that the audience didn't matter. It wasn't a question of age. Some of the very youngest kids were as scared as the oldest. And on the other hand, some of the youngest were as composed as the most veteran student.

I was curious to see whether confidence would affect their playing. Would the assured students get through their pieces without mistakes? The answer was no. Nerves surely made bad playing worse, but the absence of fear didn't make playing perfect. There was one thing that I noticed about confidence that surprised me, though. The children who looked confident recovered from mishaps faster.

I'm not always confident that everything in my day will go perfectly. I think that all salespeople understand that disappointment is simply part of the job description. But that is not to say that I am not confident about my abilities to make a sale. Like the little, squeaking violinist, I know that I'll have some off-key moments, but

I can recover and what's more, each mistake will teach me something that I can use to perform better the next time.

# SECRET SAUCE

Let's review the main points of this chapter:

Your reputation is your true business card.
Examine why a customer might want to hear from you and then deliver on it.
The motivators of a sale can guide you to form the perfect message.
However much we say, "it's just business," business is still a transaction between friends.
Challenging times provide an opportunity for you to prove yourself.
If you are not trustworthy, you will not stay in business.
Loyalty goes beyond satisfaction; it is personal.

There is great power when people come together. This chapter has emphasized relationships between buyer and seller. However sophisticated and modern we consider ourselves to be, the agreement to exchange goods and services is still very much an ancient impulse regarding trust, friendship, and loyalty.

For evidence, look at the role of a coffeehouse.

These spaces played a key role in the Middle East of the 16th century, where guests mingled without distinction of rank or creed to share ideas, exchange news and information. By the end of the 1500s, there were 600 coffeehouses in Constantinople alone. The first coffeehouses in Europe emerged in the 1600s as places for scholars, artists, journalists, political activists, to talk about how to change the world; in fact plans for the French Revolution and the American Revolution were hatched in the caffeinated atmosphere of the coffeehouse. In England, they were known as "penny universities," under the theory that for the price of a cup of coffee, a person could receive an education.

Where people meet together, there is strength. Ideas are shared and relationships form. Think of a business meeting as a potential gathering of minds to work together for a common good and shared goals.

# INGREDIENT 6
## WORK SMART

In 1756, much of the Western world was at war. Overlapping interests and antagonisms between powerful nations caused battles to rage simultaneously in Europe, North America, Central America, West Africa, India, and the Philippines. This was to be called the Seven Years' War.

Off the coast of Spain, the island of Minorca was under British rule. In the capital city of Mahon, named after Hannibal's brother in an earlier conquest, the British forces of 3,000 men were holed up in St. Philip's Castle with additional protection of a fleet of thirteen ships under the direction of Admiral John Bang. The island was strategically important because Mahon has the second deepest natural port in the world and its location at the entrance to the Mediterranean insured its possessor a distinct advantage in the region. The French attacked on April 19th with 15,000 troops under the leadership of the duc de Richelieu. Bang's strategic errors (he was later court-martialed for incompetence and executed) doomed the British Fleet, and Mahon surrendered on May 28th. The French did not lose a single man in the battle.

To celebrate, the French duke called for a lavish feast. He asked his chef to create an original sauce for seafood made of cream and eggs to mark the occasion. Scouring the island for ingredients, however, the chef could find no cream. Instead, he mixed eggs and olive oil. A new culinary creation was born. The chef called it "Mahonnaise" in honor of the French victory at Mahon.

Sometimes, when I'm slathering mayonnaise on a BLT, I think of its invention. It's a symbol of a competitive, winning spirit. On that occasion in 1756, the French confidence mirrored its achievements on the battlefield.

This chapter contains a collection of articles on the power and contagiousness of confidence in sales. Success is often a by-product of this inner fire. It asks for greatness. It deserves celebration.

# CATCH THE CONFIDENCE BUG

It's no coincidence that the most powerful speeches are those spoken in times of crisis, delivered by powerful leaders who aim to inspire. Think of George Washington's stirring plea that the destitute soldiers make one more run against the British, or Lincoln's impassioned appeal that the states remain united. The greatest orators, like Martin Luther King, Jr. and, for that matter, the thousands of high school coaches who try to rally their teams to victory against a local rival, have a common method. They portray confidence and try to instill it into their listeners.

There is something about confidence that is contagious. Even when things look bleakest, a man or woman with conviction can turn the tide in their favor. I have found this to be the case in business too. Customers require confidence. Business customers are in a state of constant anxiety about profitability, and noncommercial customers are looking for ideas that will help them be better and happier. To various degrees, they are at risk and need something to reassure them.

Salespeople who radiate confidence will find that listeners gravitate to them and trust them. It needn't be a swaggering bravado, merely a quiet steadfastness, even a calm that sends a message: there's nothing to fear because you can count on me.

Where does this confidence come from? Sales professionals need to know who they are and need to embrace what it is that makes them unique. They have to firmly believe that the thing they are selling will help the customer in a tangible way. Going back to great historic leaders, ultimately confidence has as its goal a betterment of the greater good. Washington, Lincoln, and King were not trying to line their own pockets; they wanted their people to be successful and happy and safe. In sales, if we focus on the customer's betterment, our confidence will beget their confidence. It works.

# HOW TO BE INTERESTING

Salespeople are many things, but there is one thing that we are not: boring. In my experience, a dull salesperson isn't going to be in this business very long. Customers want someone who's fun to be around. They like people who are curious and engaged, and people who are friendly, open, and positive.

However, inexperienced sales professionals sometimes make the mistake of trying to be too interesting. That is, they go overboard in talking about themselves. They try to entertain too much. It's almost like they're doing a standup comedy monologue. Ironically, that kind of bombast isn't interesting for very long. We all like the funny guy, but do we trust him? So the question is how to be interesting in a way that generates sales. Actually, it's easier than you think.

To be interesting, first and foremost is this rule: be interested. Listen to people. Ask about their lives and their work. Discover what they need, and you will uncover what they need from you.

There's no need to put on a show. Everyone wants a generous spirit, a friendly smile, a warm handshake. These are simply things. They want you to call them by name. They hope that if they're having a bad day, you can give them something to lift their spirits.

Ask yourself: What would this customer find interesting? The question sounds so basic, but it points to a winning strategy.

# ARE YOU HAPPY?

It's a simple question: are you happy? But let's not get too philosophical about it. I mean, in business, are you happy, are your customers happy, and how do you know?

Take this morning, for example. You had breakfast. Maybe you got in a car to go to work or you flipped on the television or radio to check the weather. Chances are you logged onto your computer or phone and did a bit of email correspondence. You got dressed. All of those experiences are business transactions. Perhaps they feel so routine that they don't feel like it, but each one has an opportunity to bring your customer satisfaction or dissatisfaction. Was the morning coffee fresh? Did the weatherman tell you what you wanted to know? Did your computer work effortlessly? Did your car perform right? Are your clothes comfortable?

Next step: what if those transactions were satisfactory? I'll bet you didn't write a letter to the corporations responsible for the products to thank them. I'll also wager that even if these morning transactions were less than great, you didn't complain either.

That's a roundabout way of saying that you as a consumer are probably average in expressing satisfaction. That's not necessarily good news. Statistically speaking, satisfaction is hard to determine. Only 1 out of 25 customers will complain when they're dissatisfied. Or I should say, they won't complain to the organization responsible. Instead, a dissatisfied customer will tell 9 to 12 friends about it. Conversely, a happy customer will only tell 4 to 5 people about a good experience. The majority of customers, about two-thirds, say that they don't feel valued by the businesses that serve them.

All of this points to the reality that there is a huge disconnect between our ability as sales professionals to gauge the experience of our customers and the truth about their feelings toward us. As a result, we must continually do three things: seek out feedback; nurture every business relationship; and address any negative responses immediately.

# RECOGNIZE SOME SCARY FACTS

Here are some statistics that should scare you if you manage other people. Recent studies report that the No. 1 reason employees quit has less to do with the money than people think; it's respect, or rather, the lack of it.

According to the U.S. Department of Labor, employees quit most often because they feel unappreciated. Other statistics support that sad statement: over 50 percent of employees are unhappy in their jobs; 79 percent of employees who quit their jobs said a key factor in their decision was a lack of appreciation; 65 percent of employees say that they went through the year without being recognized for their hard work. One employee summed it up succinctly, "When I make a mistake, I'm recognized 100 percent of the time; when I do something great, I'm not recognized 99 percent of the time."

Where does that leave you? Hopefully, more aware of the power of recognizing the hard work of others. There is great power in the simple act of saying, "Well done." Particularly in the business of sales, which can be a wearying profession, a little pat on the back goes a long way.

Seek out opportunities to tell others that you appreciate them. Try to catch others in the act of doing things well, and comment on it. Write thank you notes. Report on good works that you encounter to the managers of those responsible. These are small acts, and we often get so busy that we fail to see how meaningful they could be to someone else. Don't allow your sales routine to put you into isolation. You have others in your organization who support you and make your work possible. Make a determination right now that you will positively affect their work lives by showing your appreciation in sincere, memorable ways.

# MY 15 MINUTES

When the television cameras were turned on, I had a moment of panic. A few million people were going to see me on prime-time national television. Worse, I was going to be painted as the bad guy.

I was a guest on the ABC-TV show, *Jamie Oliver's Food Revolution*. In the episodes before I appeared, Oliver was trying to get healthier foods in public schools, and he had his sights set on food distributors as part of the problem. I imagined how badly it could go. I suddenly had some compassion for blindfolded prisoners awaiting execution.

And then it occurred to me that as a sales professional who worked for a large food purveyor, I didn't have anything to fear if I spoke honestly and clearly. When the inevitable accusation came, I said that we have anything our customers want. We can give them whatever they're looking for. This changed the dynamic of the conversation immediately. Then I suggested that we become partners and teammates with schools to find improved choices for the children. Oliver glowed and said, "That's the best news I could have had all day." The rest of the episode featured my company in a most favorable light.

I learned a valuable lesson that day. Rightly or wrongly, our customers form opinions of us before they know us, positive or negative. To some extent we don't have control over that. What we can manage is the truth and how it is presented. We can show what we are truly all about and let others determine whether that's right for them or not. Ultimately, a customer's choice to work with you or not hinges on their goals and your ability to help them. Focus on those two things, and as you portray yourself and your organization, respond to the customer's needs first.

# FOOD POWER

In sales, I've had a number of jobs, but for most of my career, I've been in the food industry. That's great for me because I love food. Part of the fun is the opportunity to attend events with great chefs, presidents of restaurant chains, and passionate amateurs who inspire people.

After a recent event, I had a eureka moment. I was participating in a Corporate Chef's Summit, and for a few hours, I watched, laughed, cheered, and had a ball. Some terrific people gave food demonstrations and put into words their connection to food. They made everyone in attendance understand why they care so much about their jobs. When it was over, it struck me that I felt very happy, but more than that, I felt inspired and emotionally recharged. As I analyzed those thoughts, I realized that food (not merely eating, but the associations that food encourages) is something that helps me form and focus on relationships.

Suddenly, I was hit by the realization that the power I was sensing was more than my passion for food. It emanated from the core passion itself. What I needed to do was to harness that energy and replicate it. I needed to share with others the reasons why I love food, what it does for me. In turn, they would possibly buy into it and, hopefully, that would translate to success in the sales of products and services. I have the opportunity to share my passion for food every day across the entire country. I love what I do. I wish the same for you.

Passions have changed the way we eat. The organic, sustainable revolution: It started with Frances Lappe's 1971 publication of *Diet for a Small Planet*, a then-revelatory look at the shrinking global food supply that exposed the wastefulness of using grain to produce steak instead of feeding the hungry. The vegetarian diet she proposed to ensure enough food for everyone on the planet—bulgur wheat, nuts, seeds, lentils, sunflower oil, tofu, low fat yogurt—is commonplace now, but represented fringe thinking at the time. Another believer and fellow food revolutionary is Alice

Waters, who opened Chez Panisse restaurant in Berkley in 1971, focusing on local, fresh ingredients. The first restaurant to create a position of forager, a person whose job it is "to seek out the best local ingredients and establish working relationships with farmers and suppliers," the restaurant was a trailblazer in the New American cooking movement. Waters' passion changed how America ate in the decades to follow, using organic, local, seasonal ingredients, and jump starting everything from farmer's markets and heirloom tomatoes to humane animal husbandry and sustainable fisheries.

This little truth, that sharing a passion with others is its own power, holds for any segment of the marketplace and any product. What is it that you care about? Hopefully, you are selling it or something connected to it. If so, customers will share excitement for your passion too, if you can tell, show, and project why you care about it.

# FIRE IN THE BELLY

Coming in first is a powerful motivator. Every sports fan knows this. Getting there first, whether it's the first man on the moon, the first surgeon to operate on a human heart, the first explorer to a new world, is huge. Breaking records, making history, becoming noteworthy, inventing something incredible: those things shape the world.

And yet, what happens after a person hits that huge dream? Unfortunately, history is full of tales of great moments that are followed by sad endings. It's as if people who have spent so much of their lives with the sole purpose of beating everybody else ultimately turn inward and beat themselves up.

For me, motivation is only valuable if it is sustainable. In sales, you can't have a great day and then say, "Well, I think I'll take the next week off." In my experience, the people with the most success are hungry for it all the time. There's a fire in their bellies.

Maybe it's unreasonable to perpetually expend the same kind of energy it takes to win an Olympic gold medal. I'm trying to say something different. Successes along the way are great, but they only point to a life of success when they comprise a pattern of excellence that isn't a one-time event.

In business, winning has an extra benefit. It's not a zero-sum game. When you succeed, you form relationships with others and they win too. Perhaps they get a better product, better services, or a higher level of access that helps them to prosper. Success doesn't have to come at the expense of others. And it keeps the fire burning.

# MOMENTOUS SUCCESS

"Nothing succeeds like success," wrote Sir Arthur Helps in 1868. It's more than good luck, however; success is like a magnet that draws more success to it. An author of our day, Malcolm Gladwell, has written persuasively on the idea of success. In his multi-year bestseller, *The Tipping Point*, Gladwell discusses the ingredients that turn something popular into something phenomenal. In the book, he refers to salespeople as "persuaders." It is they, he writes, who use their negotiating and communication skills to persuade others to follow.

In the business of sales, I've noticed that this act of persuasion has a curious pace to it. In the beginning, it is difficult to get a few people to follow your lead. And then momentum kicks in. With a little persistence, more and more people are attracted to the message of the persuader. To hit it really big, however, there is a point of expansion that feels like an explosion. This is the result of exponential momentum.

It's funny though how quickly momentum can shift. Not only can a fad flop and an empire crumble, but even a gradual acceleration can turn into a slow fade if you don't monitor it closely.

In the business of sales, I try to keep an eye on personal momentum. I rate myself on momentum and the energy I feel regarding it. I ask myself whether I am moving forward, backward, or stuck in neutral. There is a trick about momentum, and I caution you to pay attention to it. Sometimes, you may feel like you're moving forward, but in fact, you're really just coasting; you're slowing down, and soon your direction will change. At that point, it will take more energy to turn yourself around than if you had simply kept the good times coming.

Momentum needs to be propulsive. If you sense a slowing, fix it now. If you're feeling like you're in positive territory, ask yourself whether success can be accelerated. Either way, keep an eye on momentum.

# YOUR SALES EGO

Here's the little conversation that goes on in the head of a certain type of sales professional at the end of a botched sale, "Well, that was a disaster, wasn't it? I really messed that up. This entire week has been terrible, almost like a losing streak. A curse, really. I bet that a better sales person would have closed that deal. Maybe I'm not really right for this whole sales gig. If I can't get it together, I should look at other career options."

It's a chain reaction of negativity. Beginning sales professionals all have a conversation in their heads something akin to the above (and old pros do too, just for the record). Hopefully, they figure out that a bad day—or a bad hour—doesn't necessarily mean anything more than that.

There has to be a way for us to erect an emotional barrier between the facts of a failed opportunity and the lingering sense that we are failures. In my experience, it's a subtle, but crucial, shift that takes place mentally. It is the construction of a positive sales ego. I believe it is paramount in a profession of ups and downs like we experience, to have a strong sense of inner value. Bullet-proof self-esteem permits us to keep going, to dust ourselves off, to recall previous successes and put the most recent setback into perspective.

Our sales ego can be further fortified if we take it one step further and get into the habit of turning a negative situation into something positive and lasting. The solution is nothing deeper than an internal conversation that goes something like the following: "I guess that didn't pan out like I expected. When did it go bad? Was there a specific thing that I should have tried and didn't? You know what, the next time I should take a different approach. Oh, I forgot to mention…, that would have been a good idea. Next time I have to remember that idea. I won't make that mistake again."

# STAND BY

A while back, I made a list of attributes that I thought a great sales person should possess. It contained some familiar traits like dedication, resilience, and being goal-oriented, but I also wanted to impress on others something that I think is misunderstood in our profession. On my list, I added that sales greatness requires a sensibility of always standing by.

That "standing by" caused people to do a double take. They asked me what I meant by it. Did I mean that the job is a 24/7 thing and that we should sleep with our phones on the pillow next to our heads? Was I suggesting that we always be ready, like a marauding predator on the prowl, to pounce?

It's true that I value a fast response to customer needs (at whatever hour) and also a mindset of perpetual readiness for opportunity, but I meant something a little different by "standing by." It goes to the heart of why we are in sales. Some people think that we're in it for the money. No, that's not really it. Money is certainly a part of what we do, and it's especially prominent because of the way many in sales are compensated, but as I meet truly great sales people, I've noticed that they have something in common. They love it.

They are like the inventors who care more about the break-through than the payoff, or the sports stars who love the game so much that they'd probably play for free, if the truth were known. Sales stars love their job. And why do they love it? Because they love to serve. Their efforts are not about themselves but are focused on others. It gives them joy to serve, and they are always up for it. Another way of saying it is they are always standing by.

My question for you is a simple one: You say you love sales. Do you love the people you're selling to? If the answer is yes, then you're serving them, and that is the beginning of greatness.

# WHO'S THE BEST?

At this very minute, who's on top, the most popular, the most successful, richest, tallest, strongest? What's on the way up and what's on the way down? How does one thing in history rank with another? Good news: there are statistics for that. To find out who's the best, we can look at rankings, polls, opinions, surveys, consensus. We can find out what movie sold the most tickets over the weekend, what politician is most likely to win (or lose), what object is the most popular, and on and on. Everyone has an opinion; some people are armed with data to back it up.

At your job, on the other hand, who is the best? How is that measured? Here, it gets trickier. In our profession, rankings appear in our organizations of which salesperson had the best month or year. Even if we're not the one on the top of the board, we don't see it as a permanent commentary on our abilities. We say to ourselves, "Just watch what happens next month."

All of those statistics are a bit different from a question I want to ask, however. I mean something more essential and lasting when I ask, How do you rank as a salesperson? Are you good? How good?

To my way of thinking, there are two types of answers here: internal and external. Your internal ranking is a composite of your self-worth, your belief that you are working as hard as you can, relative to your potential, and your position in the bigger picture of the scope of your career. Externally, there are multiple indicators to tell you where you fit in. One is a result of your efforts as seen by your organization. That's the easiest number to chart. I also think there's another, equally important external mark: what your customers think of you. This is the result of making a difference in their business. Have you ever wondered how you stack up against other sales professionals with whom they've worked? If you asked your customers to give you a score from 1-10, would you be the best?

# BEING THE GO-TO

I like the phrase "the go-to." It comes from basketball. In the spring of 1985 coach John Wood, a basketball coach of Spigarn High School, gave an interview and talked about his basketball star, Sherman Douglas: "In a close game, we knew who to go to. When a game gets tough, you don't have to tell one guy to shoot and another guy not to shoot. They go to the person who gets the job done, and on our team Sherman was that person . . . the go-to man."

Everybody has a go-to person. I think it's funny how this is often completely unrelated to rank or position. Especially in business, we all know somebody who simply gets things done. When we have a question, they'll have an answer; when we need an extra hand, they're the ones to offer it. The curious thing about the go-to person is that usually it's not the head of the organization or the person with the most seniority. In my experience, it's usually the man or woman who's simply the kind of person who likes to be of use to others.

Having the reputation as being the go-to guy or gal is a smart move in sales. You want customers and potential customers to see you as a tremendous resource. When push comes to shove, you'll be the one to get the call if you are seen as being the go-to.

Be the one to care the most, to get the job done every time, to be the most trusted. If that happens, you will be indispensable to your customers, and they will tell others about you—not about your products and services, but about you.

# A SMILE SAYS IT ALL

You'll probably think I'm crazy for saying this, but the smartest thing you'll ever do is learn how to smile.

It's sort of cheesy, isn't it, to praise such a simple thing? And you might read that statement and think I intend something deeper about attitude and friendliness. No, actually. I don't. Just get good at smiling. Practice.

I read a study recently conducted in the retail market. Customers said that they were willing to pay the smiling employee standing behind the counter twice as much as someone who wasn't smiling. And it wasn't a question of having a frozen smile on their faces either. The smile only had to last for a second.

Sociologists report that our brains are programmed to respond favorably to people who smile. Their voices change when they smile and the pitch rises slightly. Our brains perceive the elevated pitch as being more polite and welcoming. All of these subconscious responses happen in a flash. Studies show that smiles are recognized, voice patterns are detected, and we sense friendliness or unfriendliness in less time than it takes to blink.

I said that you should practice smiling. I mean it. Do you know what you look like when you smile? You certainly have photographs, but it's also a good idea to stand in front of a mirror and conduct a little conversation. How natural is the smile (unlike the photo-ready frozen expression) as you talk? Your smile is an outcome of muscles, and since you control your muscles, play around with your smile. Learn how it feels to smile as you want.

A final thought—don't worry about not possessing the perfect, toothpaste commercial smile. Friends don't care about that, and if you project a warm smile to others that says you like yourself and you're open to liking other people (who probably don't have perfect smiles either), you're going to notice a surprising amount of success...and that will give you something new to smile about.

# SECRET SAUCE

Let's review the main points of this chapter:

Self-confidence inspires trust.

If you're boring, sales is the wrong profession.

Customers won't tell you if they're unhappy; they will tell others, lots of others.

Recognizing the accomplishments of others is increasingly rare.

Let passions guide your business life, too.

After a success, the momentum (the fire in the belly) will help it continue.

We all have sales egos. The trick is to keep them positive.

The best sales professional is the person who loves serving the most.

A smile is your calling card, and you can shape it to your advantage.

On a day to day basis, sales has a lot to do with motivation, and often it is self-directed. Yes, there are pressures to perform. In our industry, these benchmarks and metrics can be a lot of weight to carry. Once you become accustomed to that kind of pressure though, a sales professional's biggest challenge is how to keep up the enthusiasm, the passion, the joy of working with people. It's difficult because it is an industry that sees a lot of rejection and competition.

And yet, even with all of those challenges, I have found that people can thrive in this environment if they focus on core principles of personality. They are connected to their emotions. They radiate self-confidence and a joy of serving. They work with integrity. They thank others for their good deeds and are happy to help others. In order to survive, they develop a tough skin, but that armor never deadens their friendliness.

# INGREDIENT 7
## LOVE SALES

Who in the world doesn't love pasta? Think of all of the variations of the simple combination of flour and water and their sources in the world: not just the sauced durum wheat pastas of Italy, but couscous from Africa, spätzle from Bavaria, Asian rice-flour noodles and wontons, and dumplings, gnocchi, and so on. As a class of food, pasta is as universal as it gets.

Marco Polo claimed to have brought pasta back from China in the 13th century, but cookbooks and histories describe European dishes made with pasta centuries earlier. Arabs used dried pastas for long journeys as far back as the 5th century. For example, it is likely that they introduced dry pasta to Italy during their conquest of Sicily shortly before the 8th century. Fresh, dried, stuffed, boiled, fried, sweet, savory, from wheat flour, rice flour, or potato flour—pasta is perhaps the most-eaten food in the world after boiled rice.

There is no public service ad campaign urging people to eat pasta. It isn't necessary because it's already so much a part of our daily routine. We love it so much that pasta dishes—in all their varieties—are simply a part of living.

For the final chapter in this book, I've chosen pasta as a metaphor. What we all wish to achieve in our profession is the warmth, satisfaction, likeability, and comfort that pasta provides at the table. Just as the recipe for pasta is simple—mix together water, flour, and maybe an egg—the process to make sales success is equally simple: work hard, be likeable, and serve.

It is true that some pastas are very complex to make. The home cook isn't likely to extrude pasta dough in the shapes of macaroni, rotini, penne or rigatoni. Some pasta is easy to make and some isn't. Likewise, some sales transactions are easy and some are complex. Still, the primary concerns are the same. For the customer, the experience of a sale must be as satisfying and enjoyable as sitting down to a great plate of pasta. Sales professionals need to keep it simple, and ideas about how to accomplish that balance can be found in this chapter. Be enthusiastic and likeable. Keep a balance between your work and home life. Be resilient, smart, and positive. Find mentors who can help you. Listen. Maintain an attitude that supports fun and success.

After you finish a day with a great pasta meal (and sales success), get a good night's sleep and prepare for more tomorrow.

# RESILIENCE

*Gourmet* Magazine launched January 1941, just before America entered WWII, totally different than any other magazine on the market, none were devoted just to food. After the U.S. entered the war later that year, rationing and transportation restrictions limited what Americans could eat for the next four years. But for people who had dined at fine French restaurants before the war and for those hoping to someday, *Gourmet's* articles supplied a vicarious taste of haute cuisine. Food historian Anne Mendelson wrote: "Hardship fostered a taste for images of a happier past and perhaps a happier future." *Gourmet* continued its success over the next three decades, paving the way for other food magazines, to come on the scene, such as *Bon Appetit* and *Food and Wine*, and creating a taste for upscale food. The magazine repeatedly affirmed that being a gourmet had nothing to do with money, class or social status; it meant the food you cooked and ate should be lovingly prepared and eaten with congenial company.

In a sense, the embrace of fine food in magazines was a reaction to the challenges of war. Often, setbacks can be catalysts for unimaginable progressMcDonald's, for example, has a stellar record of turning criticism into positive change. The recent media charges of selling junk food resulted in the addition of salads to the menu, reduced fat content in hamburgers, and the cooking of French fries in healthier oil. Environmental activists who criticized the company's use of polystyrene foam in cups and containers were listened to, and an alliance with the Environmental Defense Fund resulted in use of paper products and recycling efforts that have saved 150,000 tons of waste since 1989.

Are you ready for a quiz to test your ability to bounce back from challenges? In our business, we get pushed back, people say no, and we sometimes hit a wall. The thing about falling flat, however, is that there's a bounce afterward. How well do you bounce?

Answer these statements giving yourself a grade from A to F. Then review your responses and make a plan to strengthen your weaknesses.

\_\_\_ When I think of the future, I'm optimistic.

\_\_\_ I enjoy helping people solve problems.

\_\_\_ Uncertainty doesn't bother me.

\_\_\_ I don't take myself too seriously.

\_\_\_ In a crisis, I can remain calm.

\_\_\_ In my life, I've been made stronger through adversity.

\_\_\_ I tend to find takeaway lessons in both positive and negative experiences.

\_\_\_ For me, problems are short-term issues.

\_\_\_ I don't have to be in control all the time.

\_\_\_ I have an arsenal of positive phrases to cheer me up when I need it.

\_\_\_ When someone says no, I don't take it personally.

What's your average grade? As we all know, you don't have to be an A student to succeed in sales, but you may need to be on a path of improvement. Particularly regarding resilience, you need to be able to get up, dust yourself off, and move on after you encounter disappointment. As an exercise, write down an experience when you failed at something and how you recovered from it.

# IN BALANCE

What do you do for a living? It's a trick question.

The most complete answer is complicated. You have a job, you go home, you have hobbies, you have friends, you have things you do on weekends and things you do during the week, you take vacations, you have relatives. You spend some of your time sleeping, eating, working, relaxing, thinking, getting into trouble, and just wasting time. That is to say, what you do for a living is live.

Of course, when someone asks you that question, they are asking about your professional life, but I've found that the people who are expert at living tend to be experts at work too. The reverse isn't always true, at least not over the long run.

This concept of life/work balance is becoming increasingly tough. A survey asked employees if they felt their lives were in balance regarding work and home life. The survey conducted five years ago found that 50 percent said their balance was good. Three years later, only 30 percent could say that their lives were balanced.

We all know the challenges of being wired to work and being expected to respond to every text and phone call within minutes. Most of us roll over in the mornings and the first thing we reach for is the device to check email and texts. Well, maybe it's second, depending on whether we need glasses to read.

I've discovered three points that help in the endless struggle to have it all.

First, ask yourself what are your priorities—finances, health, volunteerism, friendships, self-development? If you have a firm grasp on your values, then many of the other decisions (and distractions) are easier to figure out. When you encounter things that run contrary to your priorities, they are relegated to the bottom of the to-do list, or they are discarded altogether.

Next, determine your pace. Where are you in your life? And regarding goals, where are you in the process of achieving them? It's all well and good to be planning for retirement, for example, but what about next year? How are you planning for that?

Finally, reconcile the need to create priorities with the pace of their completion. Work/life balance is often a misalignment of values and time. By placing some of your goals in the context of where you are now in your life, you'll be better equipped to get there. In sales, you could theoretically work 24 hours a day, every day. It could consume your life. But to answer the first question, it might be "what you do" but it can't be all that you do.

# LISTEN TO ME

You can think faster than you can talk. Your brain works at a rate of about 2,000 words a minute, but you speak at only 125 words a minute. That should be a clue why listening is a challenge. Your brain wants to jump in all the time and let out some of that torrent of words it's thinking. Sales requires fast talking sometimes, and quick thinking most of the time, but it requires hard listening all of the time.

Listen to your customers. They want to be heard. Make them feel like they are important by giving them the time to have their say. Remember back to the time you were a child. When you tried to get your parent's attention, it was very important for you to have them look you in the eye, to stop what they were doing, and to let you enter the conversation. Realistically, what you said wasn't likely profound, but as relationships go, it was crucially important that they heard you.

Our sales relationships can be just like that. It isn't always a question of being efficient and getting out the information as fast as possible, and then moving on to the next customer. Instead, listening provides the opportunity for customers to explain what's going on, what they need, how they're doing, and how you can help.

In the argument of quality time vs. quantity time, our tendency in business is to lean toward quality because there are only so many hours in the day. But emotionally, people don't work that way. They need room to breathe and to feel comfortable before they will open up. If it is confidence that you are after, you have to lay the groundwork, and that foundation is paved with patient listening.

Keep these three types of listening in mind: 1) task-related—the details necessary to complete transactions; 2) relationship-related—information that informs about their life and interests; and 3) empathy-related—emotional data that connects people together.

Your customers are people, not products. They face challenges, have questions, and they need assistance. Your ability to listen will be enhanced as you put yourself in their place. They want to be heard. They want somebody to care.

# THE CHAIN REACTION OF ENTHUSIASM

At a time when Europe was the center of power in the mid-19th century, Ralph Waldo Emerson, the American philosopher and poet, was a cheerleader for all things American. He was tireless in his advocacy that there was no reason why his country and his people had to be second-place finishers in anything. He wrote, ""Enthusiasm is one of the most powerful engines of success. When you do a thing, do it with your might. Put your whole soul into it. Stamp it with your own personality. Be active, be energetic, be enthusiastic and faithful, and you will accomplish your objective. Nothing great was ever achieved without enthusiasm."

That last phrase really resonates with me, "Nothing great was ever achieved without enthusiasm." I see the powerful energy that enthusiasm brings as I meet with the people in our industry who are the most successful. There is vibrancy to their work. It is more than tirelessness; it is an attitude that there's nothing they would rather be doing. I see joyfulness in their work.

Famed chef Thomas Keller serves his signature dish at French Laundry—salmon tartare with sweet red onion creme fraiche—in an ice cream cone. Why? "People always smile when they get it, it makes them happy."

It's my opinion that others love to be around people with that kind of energy. I find it infectious to be in a room with someone who is enthusiastic about something. It doesn't even have to be a common interest of mine; it's the liveliness that makes me curious about them. I'm predisposed to like what they have to say because of the atmosphere they create.

Our motivation in sales is to make a sale, but it's also to make a difference. I keep that notion of service in the back of my mind all the time to be my anchor. As I remember the real reason I'm in sales, I find it easy to become enthusiastic as I talk and listen to people. As I do that, the people with whom I'm talking start to get excited too, like a chain reaction.

# UNDERGROUND SUCCESS

There is no way to get around the fact that success requires hard work. Many qualities contribute to the happy result, but anybody who has achieved great things made it happen with great effort.

I've been fascinated to follow the story of Tom Michaels who is doing something in Chuckey, Tennessee that no one imagined to be possible. The son of a mushroom farmer near Chicago, he received a doctorate degree studying tuber spores. After years of thinking about it, he decided to try to cultivate black Périgord truffles in the United States. He made a plan that he knew would take years to materialize. He planted an orchard of hazelnut and oak trees in the Tennessee hills (the fungus spores of truffles grow in the root systems of these trees). Next he waited. It takes several years for the truffles to appear, if they appear at all. Truffles run on their own time schedule.

Everyone thought it was impossible to grow truffles, and specifically world-class truffles, in the U.S., but ultimately that's what Michaels has accomplished. His first truffles appeared in 2007. He now has four orchards. Truffles sell for approximately $600 a pound, and Michaels is the only man in America who makes his living cultivating them.

Nobody would have blamed him for quitting along the way. They would have predicted it, in fact. In the same way, nobody would blame you for dropping out of the sales profession, which can be brutal and relentless. But Michaels was knowledgeable, passionate, and motivated. And—a big and—he made it happen by hard work.

# LIKE IT

There's sweet, sour, bitter, salty, and the fifth taste known as umami, discovered more than a century ago by Dr. Kikunae Ikeda. It's the singular taste found in the complex flavors of tomatoes, asparagus, mushrooms, cheese, meat, and other foods. As the taste of umami itself is subtle and blends well with other tastes to expand and round out flavors, most people don't recognize umami when they encounter it, but it plays an important role making food taste delicious.

Put yourself in your customers' shoes. If they can purchase the same things for the same price from somebody else—and for most of us in sales, our competitors' products and service are not radically different from our own—why should the customer buy from you? All things being equal, people purchase from the more likeable salesperson. Ouch!

Viewing likability in this light, you can see why this trait is worth mastering. Too many people in the business look at this essential skill as something innate. While it's true that some people simply seem to be inherently relatable, I've found that anyone can develop their likability muscles. For me there are four elements: being friendly, connecting to the needs and wants of others, showing empathy, and feeling authentic to others.

The topic is a bit subjective, but the bottom line is that someone responds to you and feels comfortable with you, or they don't. But why leave that chemistry to chance? Analyze yourself and make note of how people respond to you in various circumstances. When a conversation isn't working, try to decipher the moments that were destructive.

You don't have to be the class clown or the life of the party. To be likeable, you have to show qualities that others find inviting, safe, and engaging. I've noticed that likeable people—at least the ones I want to be around—have a few common traits. They are positive people. They aren't judgmental when they meet new people. They embrace new people, new ideas, and new ways of working. They radiate a sense of ease with themselves. This doesn't mean that they are perfect; in fact, likeable people are willing and able to be vulnerable and open, too. They find a way to make connections with people, either by finding values or histories that they share, or discovering common interests. And finally, likeable people are able to subvert their own needs to be the center of attention in order to showcase others.

This likeability thing is like a comfortable old sweater. Once a person embraces this trait, it becomes a warming, soothing comfort to them. The byproduct of that sensation is an enhanced ability to put others at ease too. It's less a question of formality vs. informality, but likeability is, at its heart, a generosity of spirit. You may be fortunate enough to feel that way naturally, but if not, you can reach a level that is generous by cultivating the characteristics that others find easy to like.

# THE FUNNY

Did you hear the one about the door-to-door salesman?

Jokes and sales have been teammates for centuries. I'm not talking about jokes about sales people; I mean that the ability of people in sales to employ humor to their advantage is as old as the hills. Nothing cuts through tension, establishes common ground, and puts people at ease like shared humor.

Yes, a lot can go wrong. Have you ever been in a room when somebody told an inappropriate joke? There are few things worse than that feeling of discomfort. So yes, there are things to avoid when trying to be funny, but it's a risk that has great rewards.

Sales people need to be memorable. And they need to have customers want to be around them. Humor fits the bill on both counts. An expert on workplace humor, Suzan St. Maur says that in business, make sure the joke's focus is on the situation rather than the person. Nobody wants to be singled out and made the source of a joke. For example, a joke about me tripping and falling down is different than a joke about someone else. People are willing to laugh at themselves, but when it feels like criticism, it suddenly isn't funny anymore.

Some warnings: beware of joking online. Sometimes the funny comes from the context, body language, and tone of voice. Without those guideposts, a reader is more likely to misinterpret and even to take offense.

A final thought about humor is this. Although people love to laugh, they also love to make people laugh. There's power in that. So take advantage of situations where you can make your customers feel funny themselves. Enjoy their humor, too.

# A HAPPY CUSTOMER IS A SATISFIED CUSTOMER

One of the superstars of food is Rachael Ray, somebody I've had the pleasure to meet on several occasions. I've watched her career and although she works in the kitchen and I work with different tools, I've learned a lot from her.

One of my favorite quotes of Ray's is this one: "I was raised in a household that taught us that everybody has the right to have a lot of fun." There's a joy in success. I used to think that success brought joy, as if it were some dividend that was paid to the successful after a down payment of struggle, but now I think differently. I see people who are happy in their work and those feelings make their work better. They happen in tandem and build on each other.

This happiness really can't be faked. Customers can see what is real or not. They don't expect everything to be perfect, but they do expect truthfulness. Again, Ray is exemplary here. She's the first one to say she's no great chef (she calls herself a cook, for example), "I don't want anything to separate me from the viewers. I open the cans, I chop the onions myself, and I wear street clothes. I don't want people to look at what I do and think that they can't do that, too. It's extremely important. That's why I don't wear a chef's coat. I don't even wear an apron. At home, I wipe my hands on my coat, I burn my fingers, and it doesn't look perfect. But it is my food. It's the real deal....I'm happy that way."

When I act that way, when I share the joy I get from my work with the people I serve, I think they feel happier, too. I know they are most satisfied. I like to keep three points in mind:

- I ask people if the work I'm doing is good enough and if I'm making them happy,
- I think of these business transactions as interpersonal relationships and as such, I try to nurture each one like a friendship,

- I know that sometimes, negative things happen. I embrace feedback that points me toward improvement. I find that customers are more satisfied with me when I acknowledge my shortcomings and commit to serving them better.

# A PLAN OF ACTION

I'm not perfect (shocking!) and I suspect you're not perfect either. Now what?

Well, I can't fix everything for you, but I do have some ideas on how to address your sales imperfections. The first item of business is to make a plan. Change requires a new way of addressing actions. Make an action plan that can serve as a roadmap to help you concentrate on your needs.

An action plan has five specific parts. Number one is to find an objective. In sales, you should have daily, weekly and monthly goals. But this is more than a statistic. You should visualize the end result of your labor. You need to plan the resources required as well as your limitations that will present challenges. Finding an objective should help you clarify in your own mind what it is you want to achieve.

After you have an objective, brainstorm to create an inventory of possible actions that can help you. For example, how many new contacts will you make? How will leads be generated and met? Regarding new customers, how will you interact with them? This brainstorming phase is about the possibilities out there. As you write them down—yes, make a list—don't edit yourself too much. Make notes of anything that could be a positive step for you.

Armed with a list of potential actions, it's time to create a system, an approach. Study your list and begin to prioritize which ideas might be most helpful. At this stage, don't forget to seek the advice of others you trust. Peers can be very helpful as you decide how to employ the best ideas and discard the rest.

Now you have a plan. Well, you almost have one. Take the approach that includes action items and link them in a way that creates a story of your coming success. At each step in the story, note additional steps that will need to be in place. This becomes your roadmap.

After all of this creation of an action plan, the last and most important step is about action itself. Get out there. Do it! Be aware that you may need to make some adjustments to your plan here and there as you encounter difficulties. Every journey has a few detours. Incorporate changes into the plan, that is, continue to chart your action plan as you go. This will document what's going right as well as wrong, and you'll be able to find shortcuts and avoid repeating mistakes.

# SALES SMARTS

You are familiar with the great play *Death of a Salesman*, but if you were a writer, how would you write the Birth of a Salesman? This book is full of ideas about characteristics that a sales professional should have or should develop. Here's one that I haven't mentioned yet.

Salespeople are smart. Easy to say, trickier to describe. A smart sales person is a combination of book smarts, street smarts, and people smarts. Those are three separate skills if you stop to consider them. Sales requires an understanding of business acumen, accounting, management, and analysis, but the interaction with customers draws on a separate set of knowledge: psychology, communication, and even creative writing. Sales isn't a theoretical pursuit. It happens on the street, and as such, it asks for an understanding of current affairs, sports, arts, local and national politics, history, humor and entertainment.

A salesperson is a chameleon who can shift, depending on the person who you are trying to engage. Anything that is potentially of interest to the consumer is a valid topic of understanding for the salesperson. That's a big job, it's like asking you to have an encyclopedia in your head open at all times. Still, that's exactly what sales professionals have and must have, moreover, to be successful.

It's unlikely that you know everything there is to know in the world, so the next question is simple: what to do about the gaps? I have two suggestions. First, know what your strengths are, from a knowledge base standpoint, and lead with those first. If you happen to know a lot about sports, you'll probably draw on that reservoir of information most often. Continue to add to that base of strength. Keep up to date. Try to think of ways you can use your smarts in that area to engage each customer. One's a Michigan fan, let's say, and one's an Ohio State fan. How will you talk with each of them?

Next, know your blindspots of knowledge. That doesn't mean avoid them. Quite the opposite. You don't have to be an expert to be smart; you simply have to be curious to be smart.

Let's say you have a customer who is an opera fan. And you want to have conversations with her but you don't see a way to enter a discussion about it. How about being direct and saying, "I don't know much about opera, but I know that people who love it are crazy about it. What is it about that music that makes you love it?" There's your entrance. You don't have to know everything your customer knows, but if you're smart, you can send a message that you're interested in your customer.

# FINDING ATTITUDE

Imagine that you are a casting director and you've been asked to cast the parts for a movie. One of the characters is a salesperson. In the script, she's smart, talented, and successful. But you don't have much more to go on than that. What qualities would you look for at a casting call for a salesperson?

We all know that salespeople look like anybody because we are everybody. There's no body type or height requirement to be in sales. I don't think that there are negative physical stereotypes either. Salespeople are just people…and yet….

There is a look that we have. Perhaps not a physical trait as much as a demeanor. Salespeople have a certain attitude, don't they? It's an eagerness, an internal fire, even a fearlessness. I also think that there's a joy in our attitude.

I've noticed, when I'm talking to other people how quickly I can tell whether or not someone is in sales. Maybe you've had the same experience. It doesn't take long to find out that you have a profession in common. The signs are everywhere. Here are three attitudes that jump out at me most often from salespeople.

- Sales professionals exhibit a graceful confidence. Even under pressure, they remain poised and self-assured.

- Sales professionals radiate friendliness. They are approachable physically, with a big smile, eye contact, and warm greetings. Even if they are not your friend, they act like they could be. It's an attitude of friendliness.

- Sales professionals let an atmosphere of happiness envelope them. Certainly, they have bad days too, but the attitude of being happy is like a physical reflex for them. It's a state of mind that they cultivate frequently, and it becomes their default emotional center.

The important thing to remember about attitude is that it's a choice. Unlike an inherent trait of being short or tall, thick or thin, the way we position ourselves is determined by our attitude, and that is a decision only we can make.

# MOVING ONWARD

British cookbook author Elizabeth David picked a strange time to publish *A Book of Mediterranean Food* in the early 1950s, when Britain was still rationing food. She described in great detail the Mediterranean delights she had seen—shiny fish, cheeses, the oil, the saffron, the garlic, the aromatic perfume of rosemary, wild tarragon and basil drying in the kitchen. Although she was aware that rationing would make it difficult to find the ingredients she listed, she believed her recipes were achievable, and suggested places to go around Britain that carried the necessary items. Her vision was responsible for "lifting the nation out of its culinary dark ages."

Imagine another example, being a wine producer during Prohibition. Some resourceful California wine makers made it work. Because the Volstead Act allowed for home production of 200 gallons of wine a year, an ingenious group of California grape growers sold grape concentrate, packaged it with a yeast capsule and included explicit instructions telling the customer exactly how to avoid making wine! Other winemakers shifted their business to sacramental wine, such as the Beaulieu Vineyards of Rutherford in Napa Valley, which supplied wine to the Archdiocese of San Francisco. Standards were maintained at extremely high levels, producing the finest wines possible, not skimping because it was being used for a church ritual. As a result, the company received referrals to churches across the country to supply their wine, and at the end of Prohibition, found their fine wines in much demand among San Francisco society.

I spend a fair amount of time in airplanes. With nothing much to do but sit and look out the window, I do some of my best thinking when I fly. One of the things I like to do is to observe the geography on the ground below. I like the perspective that 30,000 feet provides.

Recently, I was flying over the Rockies in Colorado. I noticed a small river below. It was mostly dried up, but it curved left and right, and it twisted past hills and into valleys. The little river cut through some steep and rocky terrain and then, over flatter ground, it made delicate switchback patterns as it edged toward the Grand Canyon.

There are many analogies that a little river like this might offer, but the one that struck me as I flew was that the river didn't seem to ever stop. Through hills, around boulders, despite a varied topography, the river found a way from its source to its destination. I could imagine a winter snowfall thawing in the spring and flowing into that river which would meander its way to something bigger and bigger still.

As a salesperson, I liken that river to the impulse I feel to never stop. Obstacles are thrown in my path, there are good economies and sour ones, people say "yes" and people say "no," but I keep moving onward.

People say "no" to us every day. It is like a potential dam of the river that threatens to impede our flow or stop us all together. But we don't stop. Like the river, we find a way around the "no." A negative response is not a personal rejection. It simply means that the way we presented our product didn't work. Any negotiation has twists and turns. It requires maneuvering. At a certain point, "no" means "no." It's time to move on to someone else. What "no" doesn't mean, at least for me, and for my little river in Colorado, and hopefully for you, is "stop."

# SECRET SAUCE

Let's review the main points of this chapter:

Resilience will set you apart from your peers.
To be sustainable, you have to work to live rather than live to work.

Brains work faster than mouths; therefore listening is a crucial skill.

Making someone happy is a reward worth seeking.

Quitting gets you nowhere.

You must be likeable, but how? Humor, fun, service are three clues.

If you know your strengths and weaknesses you can manage both.

What is a salesperson? You can create the ideal version of that for yourself.

There is no impediment that creative solutions can't maneuver.

A fitting place to end this volume is a tribute to where I started. My first week on the job in sales, as a trainee at John Sexton & Company, I heard people in the office saying a phrase over and over, "Everyone's wild about Harry." I didn't know what they were talking about, or if Harry was an actual person, but I soon found out.

Harry Panaro worked in Cincinnati. At the time I started in 1979, he was already a veteran of 18 years on the job. It wasn't his seniority that made people wild about him though, it was a combination of characteristics that I've described throughout the pages of this book.

Everybody knew Harry. Not just the owners of stores. Harry was familiar to every dishwasher in the restaurants he serviced, every mailman, every beat cop, every waitress. For him, a person's job was no indicator of status. He seemed to like everybody and be liked by everybody.

I'll never forget watching him in action. Harry always had a smile on his face, and he spent the day talking and listening to people. He was fantastic in the way he could connect people together, and his knowledge of their businesses was astounding. Often, even before they knew a problem was on the horizon, Harry knew. People trusted him, liked him, confided in him and believed him. When he gave them advice, they listened because he never steered them wrong.

Maybe more than any other characteristic, Harry was all about service. When a customer called, Harry responded immediately. It could be in the middle of the day or the middle of the night. He was there whenever he was needed. I also noticed how his view of the job extended beyond a simple business relationship. He went to his customers' kids' ball games, weddings, and graduations. His friendship continued even after some of his customers passed away. He went to funerals. He cared for the grieving.

Harry showed me, as a young sales rep, that selling is about having fun. Harry loved a good time, and the people around him had a good time when he was there. Yes, he was a walking encyclopedia of product knowledge. Yes, he was honest and trustworthy. But more than almost anything else—if it is fair to try to boil a person down into a word or two—Harry was all about "yes." He sought out agreement in others, he sold until he heard the word "yes," and when people asked him for help, there was only one response: "Yes."

I owe so much to Harry and what he taught me. He was my first go-to guy. I still talk to him and look to him for guidance. I'm wild about Harry. You can be like him. You can learn how to forge enduring relationships with customers. You can be successful and cultivate the qualities that will bring you success and happiness. It will take work, but that's what it's all about, isn't it? Yes!

# MASTERING THE SALES RECIPE
## ACTION PLAN

You have finished reading the recipe, but where are you on your personal journey toward sales mastery?

What is mastery? Below are a few definitions from merriam-web-ster.com/dictionary.
1 a : the authority of a master : dominion
    b : the upper hand in a contest or competition : superiority, ascendancy
2 a : possession or display of great skill or technique
    b : skill or knowledge that makes one master of a subject

I've also heard it defined that mastery is having mastered a par-ticular area when you are able to teach or mentor others.

I hope you have found ingredients in the book that make sense to you, and even inspire you. If you have, and they do, then it's time to take action! And in order to achieve results from those actions, you need a plan.

I have created a template for you. You can find it on the following pages to customize and make your own. I have provided suggest-ed actions and strategies around each of the seven ingredients in the sales recipe. If you have engaged in any self-development effort in the past, you know you can focus effectively on one, two or—at the most—three elements at a time. That's where you will have to do a self-analysis—reflect honestly on where you are in your sales journey; you can use the self-assessments in the book as a starting point—and prioritize where you want to invest your time. Consider how to build on your strengths as well as development opportunities.

Here is a suggested path to sales mastery.

- ☐ Read the book—one segment at a time. (You might be able to check this one off the list).

- ☐ Scan the action plan below. Note: You may have additional ideas—great!

- ☐ Establish your goal(s) for where you would like to be in 90 days. Make sure your goal or goals are specific, measurable, realistic, timely. Write them down! For extra reinforcement, share your goals with an accountability partner.

- ☐ Identify one, two, or three actions to start with. Implement them for 30 days. Document the results.

- ☐ Select one, two, or three additional actions for the next 30 days. These may be the same or different from the first ones.

- ☐ Repeat for another 30 days.

- ☐ At the conclusion of the 90 days, re-assess where you are. What have you mastered?

- ☐ Incorporate what has worked for you into the essence of who you are as a sales professional. And, as a life-long learner, ensure that what you incorporate includes always acquiring new knowledge and growing.

- ☐ Pass it on! I mentioned earlier that a master is able, and even compelled to teach or coach others. Spread the wealth. Share what you have learned. Passing it on will lift you to even greater levels of sales mastery.

☐    Enjoy!

NOTES

_____

_____

_____

_____

_____

_____

_____

_____

_____

_____

_____

_____

_____

_____

# MY SALES STORY

When did you make your first sale? (Hint: Think back to when you were a child, not just in your current professional role.) How did you feel when you made it?

_____

_____

_____

_____

_____

What motivated you to purse a career in sales? (There is no right or wrong answer and there can be more than one motivator). Examples: achievement, autonomy, competition, flexibility, money, personal growth and development, serving others, working with people.

_____

_____

_____

_____

_____

When you look over your career so far, what have been the highlights?

_____

_____

_____

_____

_____

_____

What would you like to accomplish over the next 3–5 years in your career? (If you don't have a crystal-clear vision right now, that's okay. Skip this for now and come back as the goal becomes clearer and clearer…until you can see it, think it, feel it, believe it.)

_____

_____

_____

_____

_____

_____

_____

_____

# INGREDIENT 1:
# COMMIT TO LIFELONG LEARNING

What is a topic or area that you would like to know more about and master? Commit to biting off a little more knowledge every day for the next 30 days.

Topic(s) or area(s)—include a note on how you would rate your knowledge now —beginner, intermediate, etc.

_____

_____

How I Will Learn More (e.g., reading online daily blog, listen to audio book, consult a mentor, start a master-mind group, reflect or journal).

_____

_____

Amount of Time I Will Devote to Learning Every Day (approximately—it can be as little as 5 minutes).

_____

_____

Time of Day I Will Learn Every Day (for example, if you're a "morning person," make it a morning habit).

_____

_____

_____

30-Day Learning Tracker

Note: Track your progress by just checking off each day that you met your life-long learning goal. Or write down a key fact or idea that you learned. The important thing is to track your commitment to yourself. If you skip a day—no problem. Just get back on track the next day.

| SUNDAY | MONDAY | TUESDAY | WEDNESDAY | THURSDAY | FRIDAY | SATURDAY |
|---|---|---|---|---|---|---|
|  |  |  |  |  |  |  |
|  |  |  |  |  |  |  |
|  |  |  |  |  |  |  |
|  |  |  |  |  |  |  |
|  |  |  |  |  |  |  |

# INGREDIENT 2:
# COMMIT TO EXCELLENCE

Your Excellence Attributes

1. What is something unique you bring—about you as a person or your product —to the marketplace?

_____

_____

2. What makes you memorable to customers and others?

_____

_____

3. What elevates you above your competitors?

_____

_____

My GREAT Open-Ended Questions to Build Relationships & Create Memorable Customer Experiences

This can be an individual or a team exercise—to develop a list of great questions that the competition isn't asking. Review the list regularly. As you ask questions of prospects or customers, listen carefully. Make sure your tone of voice and body language reinforce that you are actively present, and that you care about the answers and the person. Note which questions work—and which ones don't —and capture new ones you come up with. Share them with your team.

_____

_____

_____

_____

_____

_____

Preparation Is Key

When are your next three sales presentation opportunities?

| SALES OPPORTUNITY (CUSTOMER/ DATE) | GOAL BE SPECIFIC | HOW I WILL PRE-PARE TO CREATE MEMORABLE CUSTOMER EXPERIENCES | OUTCOME AND/ OR NEXT STEPS (AFTER THE PRESENTATION) |
|---|---|---|---|
|  |  |  |  |
|  |  |  |  |
|  |  |  |  |

# INGREDIENT 3:
# UNLEASH CREATIVITY

There may be people who think of sales as a technical, process-driven profession that is mostly about numbers. You and I know that it's more art than technical enterprise. A key ingredient for sales success is creativity.

There are a number of opportunities in this Action Plan to tap into creativity —telling your story, putting yourself in the customers' shoes, and building your personal brand are examples. Below are two additional areas where unleashing creativity can add up to sales.

The Best Time to Call

You have distinct questions and a creative story that inspires. You have researched the prospect. Even with all that preparation, many salespeople get nervous when calling on a new customer. Here are some creative ways to channel stress into memorable sales meetings.

☐ Check your attitude: Is it set on positive? Are you smiling? Does your body language say "friendly"?

☐ When is the best time to call? Can you identify the day and time that would be best for the customer to meet? This can require some creative common sense.
- Don't call when the person is likely to be overwhelmed, tired, or focused on issues other than your solutions.
- Do call on them when they are likely to motivated to engage in conversation with you.

☐ Where is the best place to meet? The meeting place can tell the customer a lot about you as a person and professional. The place can set the stage for a memorable encounter.

This can require some outside of the box thinking. Examples:

- Take a walk, go to the gym. Play a round of golf (is there a Topgolf venue near you? Visit www.topgolf.com) or a game of tennis, if they are athletic.
- Attend their child's sporting event – the afternoon soccer or softball game.
- Visit an art gallery, if you learn they are interested in a new exhibit.

| CUSTOMER | WHEN TO CALL (SEASON, DAY, TIME) | CREATIVE PLACE TO MEET |
|---|---|---|
|  |  |  |
|  |  |  |
|  |  |  |
|  |  |  |

Earning Referrals

They are a repeat customer and you have a growing relationship. They view you as a trusted advisor. That loyal customer is positioned to introduce you to new business.

Here are 4 ways to mine customer referrals for sales gold. If you rank high on all 4, you are in a position to earn referrals. Go for it!

☐    Prove yourself worthy. This is accomplished when you serve the customers perfectly. Provide top-notch communication and superior service before, during, and after the sale. Be creative! Go the extra mile. Turn potentially negative experiences to continued validation of your proactive thinking on your customer's behalf.

☐ Give in order to receive. I sometimes will prime the pump to get referrals. I view it as a three step process: Step #1, invite your friends and family to support your customer's business; Step #2, remind your customer that some of your friends and family stopped by and made a purchase; Step #3, now is the time to ask your business customer for another referral.

☐ Engage the new prospect respectfully. The best of all possible scenarios is when the customer makes a direct introduction to the prospect. After meeting the customer's referral, it is imperative that you engage the prospect carefully and respectfully. In a sense, you are managing two relationships in one. Be sure to properly acknowledge to your customer your gratitude for the introduction.

☐ Be prepared when it happens. Sometimes, the referrals will come out of the blue. You'll be talking to a customer and there will be the golden opportunity. The way that you respond will determine whether you seal the deal or crash and burn. In your mind, prepare in advance various responses to referrals. Make sure they are responses that highlight your commitment to the customer and your promise that you will treat the referral (who is likely a friend of the customer) with your full attention. This is where you can unleash creativity. If you can make the experience even more profitable for the customer doing the referral, the likelihood is that the referrals will keep on coming.

My Referral Responses:

_____

_____

_____

_____

# INGREDIENT 4:
# EXUDE FOOD-ITUDE

Impact of Food-itude
Who is someone you know who has a great attitude or food-itude?

_____

_____

How would you describe this person?

_____

_____

_____

_____

_____

If you have a choice of being around someone with a great attitude vs. a negative attitude, which one would you choose and why?

_____

_____

_____

_____

_____

| | MY FOOD-ITUDE ROCKS EVERY DAY, ALL DAY! IT'S NATURAL TO ME | I KNOW FOOD-ITUDE IS A CHOICE. I WORK AT IT AND USUALLY SUCCEED | IF THINGS ARE GOOD, SO IS MY ATTITUDE. WHEN THEY'RE NOT, IT'S GONE | I'M A NEGA-TIVE PERSON. I CAN'T HELP IT AND I DON'T CARE |
|---|---|---|---|---|
| Where I am now | | | | |
| Where I'd like to be | | | | |

Tip: Focus on having an authentic, great attitude/food-itude every day for 30 days. After 30 days, ask yourself:

- What difference has it made in your life?
- What has been the impact on relationships with customers and others?
- Has there been an impact on sales?

Build a Gratitude Attitude

One way to build great food-itude is to be grateful for your customers. Truly, sincerely grateful. A powerful way to show your gratitude is to acknowledge their value and thank them on business calls. To get started:

☐ Write down your customers' names.

☐ Note at least one thing that you wish to thank each one for giving you —be specific.

☐ Take the list with you on calls—or make appointments specifically to thank them.

☐ What was their reaction? Your reaction to the process?

| CUSTOMER NAME | GRATITUDE | DATE GRATITUDE COMMUNICATED | REACTIONS—THE CUSTOMER'S AND YOURS |
|---|---|---|---|
| | | | |
| | | | |
| | | | |
| | | | |
| | | | |

Benefits of Laughter

Work life can be stressful. Laughter helps to get through the tougher patches of a day. There also are a number of benefits associated with laughter.

Consider the list below and check off the benefits that you have experienced or observed. This will help you to choose laughter as an option when the going gets tough or to turn an ordinary experience into one filled with humor. Note: Make sure you always laugh with them—never at them.

☐ Laughter improves morale.

☐ Laughter helps people cope with problems.

☐ Laughter leads to creativity.

☐ Laughter makes you more alert.

☐ Laughter improves teamwork.

☐ Laughter eases stress.

# MASTERING THE SALES RECIPE

- ☐ Laughing people are more motivated.
- ☐ Laughter removes barriers.
- ☐ Laughter makes people feel less judgmental.
- ☐ Laughter makes you memorable.
- ☐ Laughter puts things in perspective.
- ☐ Laughter is healthy for your mind and body.

NOTES

_____

_____

_____

_____

_____

_____

_____

_____

_____

_____

_____

# INGREDIENT 5:
# COMMAND EXCELLENCE

Why They Buy

Why do your customers buy from you? What is it that makes the difference between what you sell and other options?

Customers are motivated differently and their motivations change over time. Sales professionals who excel tap into the motivations of their customers and can respond to them instinctively.

Below are six motivators for why customers buy. Which ones motivate your customers?

☐ It's new. Products and services that are new create a special kind of momentum. People are curious and optimistic, and these traits translate into a belief that new products are innovative and somehow better. Discovering them satisfies our curiosity.

☐ It makes me feel safe. The basic human need to feel protected often translates into sales. When people are anxious, they look for things that can help them. The action of a sale itself is all about reassurance. We communicate these values to people as we describe what our product can do for them. In business relationships, feeling safe means being profitable.

☐ It's easy. People look for ways to make their life more convenient. Businesses want to streamline and be more efficient. In both cases, the products that can, in some way, provide solutions to the ever-present issues of being overwhelmed have powerful advantages.

☐ It's cool. A sale is something like being granted entrance into an exclusive club. Owning something desirable grants status. This is as true for a sale of a multi-million dollar object to a cool new toy that sells for $1, but that every kid wants. The affiliation with something of value is, itself, a value.

☐ It makes me better. People and businesses are perpetually looking for ways to improve. They want to amplify what they already have with something that sets them apart and makes them better, smarter, faster, stronger, more …

☐ It will help me win. This motivator is simple. We all want to win, and we are drawn to products and services that give us an edge.

Integrity and Excellence

How long does it take to build trust? If you're like most people, your experience demonstrates that it can take a while to earn the trust of another person.

How long can it take to break trust? One second.

"Your word is your bond" is a well-known saying. Keeping your word is about integrity. Integrity is about being honest. If you want to be known as a person who cares about what you say and do, you are committed to a life of integrity.

Looking back over the last 30 days, how often did you do or say what you promised?

☐ Always

☐ Almost always

☐ Sometimes

☐ I don't keep track

If you didn't answer "always," here are a few tips.

- Think before you promise something – no matter how big or small it seems to you at the time, it could be extremely important to the other person.

- When you do make a promise or say you will do something, write it down. Align it with a day and time when you will do it, and make sure the commitment and deadline are clear to the other person.

- If something happens to prevent you from keeping your commitment, let the other person know as soon as possible. Then set a new deadline if the promise is still relevant.

More than Loyal

Most of us have had experience with "customer satisfaction" surveys. Here's what the research shows: customers who say they are "satisfied" or "very satisfied" are not likely to be, or become, loyal customers.

Customers who self-identify as "loyal" note that they feel an emotional connection to the brand and/or to you as a sales person.

A key to loyalty is a customer's level of engagment. Toward this end, how do you rate yourself on the following statements?

| STATEMENT | STRONGLY AGREE | AGREE | DISAGREE | STRONGLY DISAGREE |
|---|---|---|---|---|
| 1. I am passionate about my work and I continuously attempt to make a strong connection with people regarding products and services. | | | | |
| 2. I work hard and I put in my time, but there's a big chunk of my day when I coast along. | | | | |

| STATEMENT | STRONGLY AGREE | AGREE | DISAGREE | STRONGLY DISAGREE |
|---|---|---|---|---|
| 3. I am unhappy more frequently than happy at work. I tend to complain a lot, and I'm not as productive as I probably should be. (Yes! This ties back to food-itude.) | | | | |

If you answered "Strongly Agree" to the first statement, you likely earn loyal customers. If you answered in any other way, you have work to do on the way to loyalty and excellence.

# INGREDIENT 6:
# WORK SMART

Working Smart builds on Ingredient 5 in the sales recipe—Commanding Confidence. Confidence is contagious. Customers require your confidence. Your confidence will lead to their confidence.

Your Personal Brand

Where does confidence come from? Sales professionals need to know who they are, what they stand for, and what makes them unique. This is your opportunity to build your confidence and your personal brand. Through the three steps below, you will develop tools to build your brand. Use the one word and value statement in your email signature, voice message, all over social media. Use the story in conversations and presentations.

What do you stand for in one word? What is your passion? Examples: caring, committed, competent, creative, customer-focused, dedicated, detail-oriented, determined, dominant, efficient, fearless, friendly, generous, inspiring, innovative, insightful, knowledgeable, persistent, positive, resilient, resourceful, sincere, trustworthy, unstoppable.

My one word: _____

What is the value you offer in about 6 words? What makes you the go-to person? Example: Solutions to improve health and wealth. Training and tools to improve employee engagement. Technology to build your personal brand. Your personal value statement should tie to your one word.

What is your personal story that can help and inspire others as well as build your brand? In the beginning of the book, I shared my story—"A Tale of Two Passions." In the beginning of these planning pages, I asked about your sales story. This story can build on that. It should also build on the one word and value statement above. Keep it short. People remember stories. Tell it so that others can relate and learn from it.

Here are a few questions that can help guide your story.
- What is a goal that you achieved?
- What obstacles did you have to overcome?
- When did you turn a negative into a positive?
- What results have your realized for others?

My Sales Story:

_____

_____

_____

_____

_____

_____

_____

_____

_____

_____

_____

# INGREDIENT 7:
# LOVE SALES

As I meet truly great salespeople, I notice that they have something in common. They love sales. Stars in our profession love their job because they love to serve. It gives them joy to serve, and they are always up for it.

Do you love the people you're selling to? If the answer is yes, then you're serving them, and that is an essential part of the journey toward sales mastery.

Are You Resilient?

No matter how much you love sales, we all face rejection, push back, and sometimes we hit a wall. The thing about falling flat, however, is that there's a bounce afterward. Think of a time when you fell flat. How did you recover? What did you learn?

When I fell flat:

_____

_____

_____

_____

How I recovered:

_____

_____

_____

_____

---

What I learned:

_____

_____

_____

How Well Do You Bounce?

Give yourself a ranking of 1-10 for each of the following statements. Then choose two strengths and one developmental opportunity to focus on when times are challenging over the next 30 days.

_____ When I think of the future, I'm optimistic.

_____ I enjoy helping people solve problems.

_____ Uncertainty doesn't bother me.

_____ I don't take myself too seriously.

_____ In a crisis, I remain calm.

_____ I grow stronger through adversity.

_____ I tend to find takeaway lessons in both positive and negative experiences.

_____ For me, problems are short-term issues.

_____ I don't have to be in control all the time.

_____ I have an arsenal of positive phrases to cheer me up when I need it.

_____ When someone says no, I don't take it personally.

Two Strengths:

One Developmental Opportunity:

In Balance
   What do you do for a living? You're thinking, "I'm in sales." Yes, sales is your professional life. You also have a life outside of our profession. You go home, you have friends and family, you have hobbies. You sleep, eat, relax, think. What you do for a living is live.
   The concept of work/life balance can be tough to achieve. There are three points, if you consider them  seriously, that can help you live a life of having it all.

1.   What are your priorities? What are your values? When you make decisions aligned with your values, your life tends to be in balance. Examples: volunteering, financial security, health, time with family, self-development.

My priorities/values:

2. What is your pace toward your goals? Establishing goals is one of the first steps in the Action Plan. If you wrote down, SMART goals, are you satisfied that your daily thoughts and actions are moving you toward achieving them? If you didn't write down goals, do you have greater clarity now?

3. Are your priorities/values and pace aligned? Work/life balance is often a misalignment of values and time. In sales, you could theoretically work 24 hours a day, every day. It could consume your life and then over time the love for your job could fade away. Back to the question: what do you do for a living? Sales might be what you do, but it can't be all you do.

---

MY 90 DAY SMART GOALS:

START DATE: _____  END DATE: _____

MY ACCOUNTABILITY PARTNER: _____

MY SIGNATURE: _____

| 1ST 30 DAY DATES | ACTIONS | OBSERVATIONS/ RESULTS |
|---|---|---|
|  |  |  |

# MASTERING THE SALES RECIPE

| 2ND 30 DAY DATES | ACTIONS | OBSERVATIONS/ RESULTS |
|---|---|---|
|  |  |  |

| 3RD 30 DAY DATES | ACTIONS | OBSERVATIONS/ RESULTS |
|---|---|---|
|  |  |  |